The Power of Darkness

The Power of Darkness

SERMONS FOR LENT AND EASTER
(SUNDAYS IN ORDINARY TIME)

DURWOOD L. BUCHHEIM

SERIES C GOSPEL TEXTS

C.S.S. Publishing Company, Inc.
Lima, Ohio

Copyright © 1985 by
The C.S.S. Publishing Company, Inc.
Lima, Ohio

5852 / ISBN 0-89536-746-7   PRINTED IN U.S.A.

Table of Contents

[1] Common Lectionary
[2] Lutheran Lectionary
[3] Roman Catholic Lectionary

Matthew 6:1-6, 16-21 (Common, Lutheran)   Ash Wednesday
Matthew 6:1-6, 16-18 (Roman Catholic)

Spirituality Made Simple?

For many of us, the religious experiences of other Christians look much more attractive and exciting than our own. Because of this dissatisfaction with our own spirituality we are in some danger of becoming spiritual-chondriacs. We're forever taking our spiritual pulse and temperature. We're running to this or that spiritual doctor or hospital. It can result in a bandwagon spirituality. Whatever happens to be selling at the moment, we want to buy. Mark Twain tells the delightful story about the cat who sat on a hot stove lid. He said the cat would always remember that experience and never sit on a hot stove lid again. But he went on to say, neither would the cat sit on a cold one! The lesson being, that sometimes we read into an experience more than is warranted.

That is easy to do with the term "spiritual". More than one pastor in our district has received a thumbs down vote by an interview committee because he or she was not "spiritual" enough. The word spiritual carries a great deal of baggage. For some it has become a code word denoting acceptance or unacceptance because of words, hairstyles, dress, and a certain kind of Christian "style". For some, being spiritual is the same as being anti-intellectual. For others it's a putdown concerning social involvement, a serious attempt to divide life into sacred and secular compartments. For some, spirituality has become identified with a pietistic jargon or participation in certain kinds of religious experiences. I like the realism of the Baptist preacher Clyde Fant when he wrote:

We have all sat through almost unbearable services where absolutely nothing happened at all except mutual back-slapping,

8

endless hello-saying, and vigorous head-nodding. If an idea walked into the room it would be voted down. In these services, the highest good is imagined to be a group sitting in a friendship circle, holding hands, smiling vacuously, and singing "Bless Be The Tie That Binds." People may become very enthusiastic after one of these services in which nothing was said that they did not already know and had not already heard a thousand times before. Particularly if it was what they wanted to hear and if it was said more fervently than usual, "Wasn't that great?" But if asked what was so great, "I don't know, but wasn't that the best you ever heard?"[1]

Preacher Fant's words provide a good introduction to our Ash Wednesday text. The words "Beware of practicing your piety before men in order to be seen by them" (6:1) come as a jolt to the devout. The Greek word translated as "religious duties" or "piety" or "spirituality" is also the word for "righteousness." This particular text, peculiar to Matthew's gospel, is found in the middle of the famous Sermon on the Mount. The term righteousness, if not the central focus of this unique Sermon, is certainly one of the key thoughts. The German theologian Jeremias sees Matthew 5:20 — which reads, "Unless your righteousness (or piety or spirituality) exceeds that of the Scribes and Pharisees, you will never get into the Kingdom of Heaven" — as the main theme of this highly structured and familiar sermon."[2]

But in our text we receive a sober warning concerning these spiritual acts of devotion. Martin Luther is given credit for this observation concerning human nature: "I am more afraid of my virtues than my vices." Centuries ago Jesus Christ said something similar in these words: "Beware of practicing your piety before men in order to be seen by them." (v. 1) Here is our Lord's warning concerning the strange truth that we can get into serious trouble through doing that which is good.

The first spiritual discipline we are warned about is that of alms giving. "Thus, when you give alms, sound no trumpet before you, as the hypocrites do in the synagogues and in the streets." (v. 2) This is the sort of giving you do when the TV cameras are on you and you make the evening news! It is like being an actor in a play and one's giving is turned into a performance. And, of course, it is a performance that is geared to boost one's own spiritual stature. In the New Testament, "hypocrite" is a powerful word. It means being a phony person, a person who is a sham or counterfeit. Jesus defines it well when he warns against the dangers of Pharisaism in these words: "The scribes and the Pharisees sit on Moses' seat; practice and observe whatever they tell you, but not what they do; for they preach, but do not practice." (Matthew 23:2-3) It is the appearance of spirituality without the substance of it.

The left/right-hand illustration demonstrates that the kind of charity God appreciates is that which is done with little thought for recognition in the parish newsletter or on a fine gold plaque. But spirituality can easily turn into a form of self-display: and when *that* happens, that is *all* that happens. "We have received our reward." (v. 2) It is like receiving a business receipt marked "paid in full." This is God's judgment on charitable giving that is handled like a commercial transaction.

Our second example of spirituality is that of prayer. Prayer was an important and vital power among the spiritual people of Jesus' day. One would think that, of all our spiritual practices, something so personal and private as prayer, would be incorruptible. But such is not the case. The people who were judged "spiritual" people in Jesus' time observed set times for prayer. If, during those prescribed times for prayer, you happened to be on the street corner, your praying would receive the praises of numerous spectators. In contrast, God-approved praying is that which is done in private. Now too many of us feel most comfortable with this advice on where to pray. But we who are timid and self-conscious about praying publicly, and who are excessively worried about "what people will think," need to be reminded of the old principle which calls us "to show when tempted to hide; to hide when tempted to show." Public praying is not the issue here. It was praying to receive people-praise that received God's judgment. "They have already been paid in full." (v. 5)

The final illustration in this list of important spiritual duties is that of fasting. Fasting was a sign of penitence. The very spiritual people usually fasted on Monday and Thursday. As we know, some of the prophets already had their problems with this spiritual practice. The prophet Zechariah summed it up in the pointed question to the spiritual people of his time: "Was it for me that you fasted?" (7:5) We hear overtones of the same concern in our Old Testament lesson for today, where the prophet Joel warns us about "rending garments and not hearts." The warning remains timely. We can fast in order to lose weight; or because it is the thing to do (especially during Lent); or as a method to get God on our side. It is also a good way to call attention to how "spiritual" we really are. This human desire was somewhat innocently expressed by the confirmation student who asked, "What's the point of doing something spiritual if nobody knows you are doing it?" It comes to the fore in the discipline of fasting. Obviously, fasting has to show. So we have the mysterious reference of "disfigured faces" — faces that had spiritual suffering spelled all over them. Such visible spirituality brought the praise of admiring spectators — and the old refrain, "they have received *their* reward." (v. 16)

Human applause is strong medicine. That is surely one obvious lesson coming out of our text. We all like to be affirmed and complimented, especially where our spirituality is concerned. In our desire for spiritual experiences and spiritual growing let us not forget our vulnerability to the power of people-praise. The temptation to make a show out of our spirituality, as well as to judge others by our style of spirituality, is a strong one. Jesus' warning is clear. What matters most with God is the honesty with which we exercise and exhibit our spirituality.

But our text does not forbid spiritual actions. God is not against being spiritual! The clear words of one who practiced what he preached, Dietrich Bonhoeffer need to be heard again:

> By practicing self-control we show the world how different the Christian life is from its own. If there is no element of ascetism in our lives, if we give free rein to the desires of the flesh (taking care of course to keep within the limits of respectability), we shall find it hard to train for the service of Christ. When the flesh is satiated it is hard to pray with cheerfulness or to devote oneself to a life of service which calls for much self-renunciation. (page 146, The Cost of Discipleship, Dietrich Bonhoeffer, Macmillan, New York, 1956).

But there is tension here, between what Jesus says in chapter five and what he is saying in these opening words of chapter six. We are to let our light shine. We are to get the salt out of the shaker and the light from beneath the bushel basket, so that people might see our Christianity. This concern about the misuse of spiritual disciplines is no call to an invisible nor undisciplined Christian life. Nevertheless, our Ash Wednesday gospel raises some serious questions. Do we use free prayer as a way of establishing ourselves as a spiritual person of great piety? Do we give to the poor as a way of receiving recognition for our spirituality? How much of our spirituality is of the self-seeking kind? These are useful questions for us to think about.

But as we face these questions, can any of us say that we always give, or pray, or fast out of pure and positive motives? Even if we redouble our efforts, would that do it? Sometimes that is what we try to do, especially during the Lenten season. There is nothing wrong — and there is a lot good — about this critical look at our own spirituality. We may well discover a great deal of spiritual thinness in reference to our spirit. But spiritual health does not come with navel-gazing nor with running after this or that spiritual medicine show. Here I like the wise and calm counsel of Joseph Sittler, who said, "You find that your self emerges more quickly if you do not keep scratching the question."

What if being a spiritual person is not as complicated as we are prone to make it? Could it be that in this passage we have spirituality made simple? It *is* simple, because its recognizes that faith does good works naturally and spontaneously, like a good tree producing good fruit. Remember, this text is a portion of the Sermon on the Mount. Remember that the concept of "righteousness" (or piety or spirituality) is one — if not the main — theme of this sermon. Our spirituality, the sermon tells us, is to be better than the spiritually elite of that time (Scribes and Pharisees). Their spirituality was pointed in the direction of keeping the law. Our Lord Christ calls for more than this. Our lives are not to be shaped so much by law as by God's love. God loves by letting his rain falling on the just and unjust alike. That is the kind of love that shapes, forms and motivates our lives. Here is the spirituality or righteousness that exceeds that of the Scribes and Pharisees. It is the practice of love. It is a love which corresponds to God's love. It results in a life that seeks God's righteousness and not one's own. His love doesn't remain invisible in our lives. Rather, it is made visible in our giving, praying and fasting. But these things are done not for self-display nor to add another "star in our crown." Rather, they come forth naturally and spontaneously. We don't have to use acts of love to build ourselves up. We are free to love in God's love. In fact, we can't keep it bottled up. It breaks out and touches the people around us. In this freedom we give because people need our help. Isn't that simple? In this freedom we pray because God wants us to pray? Isn't that simple? In this freedom we exercise self-discipline because it is good for us. There is nothing here about "making spiritual points" or climbing the "spiritual ladder". We are free to give, free to pray, free to do because it is needed — not because we have to get a passing grade in spirituality. And, praise the Lord, we no longer have to compete in that depressing, judging contest of "Mirror, mirror on the wall, who is the most pious of them all?" And, who knows? In this great freedom we may even discover that it is more helpful for us to read fewer "how-to" spiritual books and more "what happened" history books! For a sense of history brings with it a sense of realism, and to lessen the tendency to push panic buttons and follow spiritual fads.

So spirituality is more likely to happen if we use this meaningful season not just to reflect on the temperature of our spirituality but by recalling and remembering the steadfast and faithful love of God. The exercise of such simple spirituality may not get you on a talk show. But never mind. God's promise of his reward is still there. His reward is not in our becoming more spiritually prestigious but rather in our relationship with him.

In that relationship (if the experience of the saints of old tells us anything) the continuing rewards come as surprises. Sometimes they come in the surprise of satisfaction and sometimes in the surprise of more giving, more praying and more fasting! Here is spirituality made simple, but also made satisifying. In this spirit — and in this promise — we once again make our journey to Easter. Amen

1. Clyde Font, *Preaching For Today,* (New York, Harper and Row, 1975).
2. Joachim Jeremias, *Sermon on the Mount,* (Philadelphia, Fortress Press).
3. Dietrich Bonhoeffer, *The Cost of Discipleship,* (New York, Macmillan, 1956), p. 146. Reprinted by permission.

That's the Way Life Really Is!

Some time ago the Evening News pictured the dramatic action and interaction among a group of teenagers who were suffering with incurable cancer. The fact that they who were being filmed and interviewed are now dead, made the story even more compelling and powerful. In one interchange the conversation went something like this.

Young woman to young man: "What's the first thing you are going to do when you get to heaven?"

Young man: "I'm going to ask God why he put me through so much trouble and then I am going to punch him in the nose!"

Contrast that scene with the commercial that puts you on a beautiful beach in front of a boiling pot of lobsters with a can of beer in your hand and saying, "It don't get no better than this."

Have you ever been tempted to chuck this whole Christian business? If you made a decision today, to no longer be a Christian, what changes would take place in your life? Would tomorrow be much different than other Mondays? What about next week or next year? One thing that would be different for me is that I would lose my job. For those who teach at a Seminary, or serve a parish, there is that added incentive to believe!

But if we decided there wasn't anything to this "God-business" any more, would the only discernible change be that (1) we wouldn't have to get up on Sunday morning and that (2) we would have a little more money to spend on other things.

Do things go better with Christ? Can we point to specific Christian results?

Jesus had just been baptised. There is mystery surrounding the reason for Jesus' baptism, but it was a significant event because it marked the beginning of his ministry. Most of us understand it as a kind of commissioning or ordaining service where Jesus received the promise, "You are my beloved son in whom I am well pleased."

But the first result of that promise is trouble! And just when things were beginning to fall into place and coming together; just when that which he had been preparing for — his messianic ministry to God's people — at this significant moment the same Spirit who called him "beloved" ordered him into the wilderness to be tempted by the devil. "And Jesus, full of the Holy Spirit, returned from the Jordan, and was led by the Spirit for forty days in the wilderness, tempted by the devil." (vv. 1-2) This doesn't read like the beginning of a three-act play which sets us up for the inevitable happy ending. As Israel, the "old Son of God" was tested through forty years of wilderness wandering, so also there is struggle for Jesus Christ, the new Son of God.

Struggle it is! The "tempting" going on here is something more than taking a forbidden trip to the local tavern or sneaking a look at some dirty pictures. What is going on here is not so much enticement to sin as it is a struggle, a confrontation — a *test* to reveal what a person is made of. It is a test engineered by the prince of darkness, the ruler of organized evil. And it takes place in the wilderness. The wilderness is not just a pleasant place to take canoe trips. It is not a vacation spot, but rather a place of contrasts: rich fertile soil made barren through the lack of moisture; burning sun in the daytime and bitter cold at night. It is not the kind of place you go to "get away." Jesus is tested in the place of loneliness, fear and danger. He doesn't get to enjoy or savor the experience and promise of his baptism. He goes from the mountaintop on Sunday to the wilderness on Monday.

Is this perhaps a one-shot test? Is it a temporary test, on-the-job-training that will lead to a promotion and better things? Sorry! The concluding verse gives us little comfort: "And when the devil had ended every temptation, he departed from him until an opportune time." We know that immediately following this wilderness experience, Jesus went to his home town to preach and to witness and it nearly cost him his life. For Jesus, testing is followed by more testing.

In 1972, Kent Knutson, who was then President of the American Lutheran Church, was one of the "centennial-celebration" preachers at the church where I was pastor. In his fine sermon on that warm summer morning he shared this personal story:

> *On the Saturday before Easter I and my family got up early to visit my mother who lives in a small town in Iowa. She is eighty-two years old. She is in ill health. We expect that she will die soon. For this she is quite ready. In reality the Knutson family went to see her to say their good-byes. While we were visiting with her we received the sad news that my sister's young son had a terminal illness. That was some very sad news that had to be shared. Late that evening we returned to Minneapolis. It had been an emotional day for us. The next day was Easter. That was a great day for the entire Knutson family. Early on Monday morning we took our daughter to the bus so she could return to Luther College. At 1:00 p.m. the call came. The bus had overturned and some of the students were injured and several had been killed. At first we thought it was our daughter who had been killed in that tragic accident. But within a few hours she was able to get to a phone to assure us that she was all right.*

Kent Knutson concluded this personal story with this insightful observation: *"And that's the way life really is!"* On December of that year, our congregation brought its centennial celebration to a close in a moving, festive service. During that combined, eventful service taped excerpts were played from previous Sunday services. Once again were heard Kent Knutson's ringing words, "And that's the way life really is!" But when we heard them this time, he was fighting for his life in a Rochester hospital.

"That's the way life really is!"

It makes a wonder about this "Christian business." There seems to be a considerable gap between expectations and experiences. The older I get, the wider the gap. Now every physical examination threatens to become a kind of wilderness experience. "Is the Lord among us or is he not?" The people asked that of Moses as one thing after another was happening to them. There, again, is the popular but persistent bottom-line question: should not our faith in God have its payoff?

I would like to suggest that this story, of the testing of Jesus, is our story too; that, indeed, this is really the way "life really is" and that means the Christian life. There is that therapeutic approach whereby we tend to adapt, ignore or explain away the tragedies that happen around us or to us. Hans Kung, the popular and well-known

Catholic theologian, writes these words: "Here we are at the very roots of the question of being human and being Christian; coping with the negative side of life is the acid test of the Christian faith."[1]

To be human is to be tested. The Bible is a book of testing from beginning to end. It begins with the test in the Garden of Eden and ends with the great hour of tribulation. As already noted, this was the experience of our Lord. There were exultation and struggle, mountains followed by their valleys. This is the rhythm of real living. "Sometimes I'm up and sometimes I'm down." The old Negro spiritual tells it ike it really is: "Nobody knows the trouble I've seen, nobody knows but Jesus."

If this story of Jesus' testing means anything, it means we dare not put God to the test, which means we live by God's promises and not his guarantees. Implicit in all three of Jesus' tests was the fundamental basic temptation to become the kind of Messiah everyone could easily recognize. So life does not become for the believer a kind of supermarket where we can get anything we want. That would be to live by "bread alone."

It would mean keeping a Christian "scorecard" which, when added up, proves that it pays to be a Christian. It sounds un-American, but I would suggest that this year, as we once again make our way to Easter, it would be well for us to examine our tendencies to overmagnify the power and bliss of our faith. Do we tend to claim for it more than is true — maybe even more than it can deliver? It might be well for preachers to be reminded of the danger of over-promising in reference to Spirit results. We remain saint and sinner, a combination of the old and new "Adam," dealing not only with the power of grace but also of sin. In the Bible, as well as in life, there is a "modesty" about the power of the Gospel we should see and heed.

This also means there are no easy solutions to some of the problems we face today. How do you think Jesus would respond to the manufacture of nuclear bombs? What kind of stand would he have made on the Viet Nam War? Would he come out for censorship in regard to pornographic material? This is not a call to avoid these issues. Certainly some stumbling, confusion, disagreement, and frustration should be anticipated as we attempt to discover God-pleasing solutions.

We are being tested. Christians are tested. Tests are not always comfortable or comforting. But they are useful. They reveal what we are made of. In our text they revealed a Jesus Christ who resisted shortcuts to a popular ministry and remained faithful to the promises of God.

He came to *be tested,* not to put *God* to the test, and his ultimate test was death upon the cross. Here the testing of our Lord is finished. The great victory has been won. Never again can the evil one test Christ as in the wilderness. Jesus is now the living Lord. But we know that for us the testing is not over. Evil remains. The struggle between flesh and spirit goes on. But in our text, every time Jesus was tested, he came through by using the sword of the Spirit which was the Word of God.

Here is our power. God, through his Word, does not insure faith, but he *enables* it — he makes it possible. "We have a high priest who can sympathize with our weaknesses. He has been tested in many respects as we have, yet without sinning." (Hebrews 4:15) Yes, we live in a world of struggle, suffering and sin. "That is the way life really is." But we have Christ with us, because we have the Word with us. It is the Word which carries this great promise in all our testing: "Let my grace be sufficient to you, for my strength is made perfect in weakness."

Let us Pray:

There are varying pathways
Of sunshine and shade.
All of it grace,
Be not afraid.

Amen

---

1. Hans Kung, *On Being a Christian,* (New York, Doubleday and Company, 1974), p. 571.

Luke 13:31-35   *Lent 2 (Common, Lutheran)*

Prophet, Pulpit, Pew and Politics[1]

The date is 608 B.C. Good King Josiah is dead. It is the beginning of the reign of Jehoikim. He was placed on the throne by the Egyptians. For the people of God it is a time of political uncertainty. Assyria is no more. Egypt is not a friendly ally. The powerful country of Babylonia is beginning to flex her muscles. So for the people of God it is also a time of anxiety. Security seems to be their top priority. The Temple has become very popular. (This is not the first nor the last time that the church has become popular in time of stress.) The attendance percentage is way up! At this time, preaching between the inner and outer courts of the Temple, is the prophet Jeremiah.

The content of Jeremiah's sermon is found in chapter seven of the Old Testament book named for him. It is blunt and hard-hitting. He does not affirm the churchgoers on their faithful attendance, their offerings or their sacrifices. Instead, they hear the ringing — and stinging — words, "Amend your ways and your doings." (7:3) The sermon deals with this central question: What gives people protection and safety? Priests and prophets answered that protection comes through the Temple and its sacrifices. Jeremiah said that genuine protection can only come through moral living. He accused the people of making a "protective charm" out of the Temple. They should not expect that their "religious activity" would cover their irreligious lives. No magic. No holy words. No formulas. The unrighteous shall not inherit the Kingdom of Heaven. Security comes only through transformed living.

Jeremiah was a realist. He not only told his people that times were bad, but that they would get worse! The strength and vitality of Judah were being corroded by self-indulgence and vanity. The Prophet agonized over his country's sickness. But many of the people preferred to listen to spiritual quacks who cried "Peace, peace!" when there was no peace. People put their trust in ritual and religious rigamarole, but that was like so much holy ointment being spread on a malignant cancer. What it did was to encourage a complacent attitude. Truth became a forgotten virtue. People were like "well-fed lusty stallions each neighing for his neighbor's wife." (5:8) They showed little concern for the poor and defenseless victims of society. Blind nationalism was running wild.

This is what the prophet saw when he looked upon his own society. Prophets were not so much future-looking, but they were pretty sharp in reading the "signs of the times." They saw that which people like to forget, the vital connection between righteous conduct and a secure people.

God could get along without the Temple, just as he survived without the sanctuary of the Ark of Shiloh (eighteen miles north of Jerusalem) many years before. In the days of Eli and Samuel that was probably the holiest place in all Israel. Nevertheless, Jeremiah's sermon, predicting the destruction of the Holy Temple, is highly unpopular. It was too negative and too political. And, of course, it was simply unthinkable. God wouldn't let something like that happen to his people. So the sermon aroused great resentment throughout the congregation. So serious was the reaction that even a call to another place would not satisfy. The death sentence is demanded. The trial is held. Jeremiah makes his defense, without retreating an inch. (vv. 12-15) Members of the royal household and other high authorities were impressed by the courage of this preacher. Like the Roman Governor, Pontius Pilate, centuries later, they found no fault with Jeremiah that was deserving of the death penalty.

In this particular confrontation this prophet comes out the victor. But the tough, bitter times for Jeremiah are immediately ahead. He will have decreased support and will more and more become like that proverbial "voice in the wilderness." His courage and faith did not enable him to escape suffering; rather, it increased it. In his own humanness we see timidity, coupled with depression and the desire to give up, along with cries of pain and vengence. Yet this prophet of God persisted. He continued to challenge the idols of his day, whether they be found in the church or the government. He persisted because he believed the Lord called him to be a prophet.

It is well that the church in her wisdom has linked together this passage from Jeremiah and the gospel lesson from the thirteenth chapter of Saint Luke. Both passages emphasize the importance of prophets and the whole matter of "prophetic preaching." But even beyond this, there are significant similaries between Jeremiah and Jesus. I doubt if there is another Old Testament person who more closely resembles the life of Jesus than Jeremiah. They came from small villages and neither were highly regarded by the home-town folks. They both experienced an intense, personal relationship with God. Their messages were not always positive and affirming. In his day, Jeremiah preached that unless the people of God "ceased their violence against the alien, the fatherless and the widow . . . this house shall be forsaken." (Jeremiah 22:3-5) In our gospel, in his lament over the holy city of Jerusalem, Jesus says the same thing: "Behold, your house is forsaken." (v. 35) They had similar historical situations. They confronted the establishment, both religious and political. Both were misunderstood. Both suffered and their earthly lives ended in failure. But, more important for our purposes on this day, both were regarded as prophets.

In our text, the prophet Jesus has to deal with the government. The warning from the Pharisees (which also indicates that not all Pharisees were against Jesus) indicates that Herod Antipas, the King of Galilee, who murdered John the Baptizer, is becoming disturbed about the disturbing presence of Jesus. But like Jeremiah he doesn't back off. The truth needs to be spoken. "Go tell the fox that I am going to do what I have been doing and what I have to do." (v. 32)

There is the story told of Hugh Latimer, an English Reformation martyr, who was preaching in the famous Westminster Abbey, when King Henry was in the congregation. In the pulpit (and having seen the King), the preacher thought to himself, "Latimer! Latimer! Latimer! Be careful what you say. The king of England is here!" Then he went on. "Latimer! Latimer! Latimer! Be careful what you say. The King of kings is here."[2]

True prophets fear God more than governments or votes of popularity.

Prophets are to be found not only in the pulpit but also in the pew. But they need to be *found!* This whole issue is one in which congregations should become involved. It's a cop-out to take care of the whole matter by "keeping politics out of the pulpit." We hear that all the church needs to be concerned about is the conversion of sinners. If the problem is drinking, convert the drunk. If the problem is prostitution, convert the woman. (Not much attention is given to the man by the way!) But what about the problem of greed? What about the matter of hate? We who claim to be long-time Christians, are we free from the power of greed and hate? Which do you think is most destructive in our society, drinking or greed? It is in this reality that the church needs to talk about equality, freedom and justice. This is especially true for us who are the comfortable ones. In our sinful nature we tend to go to and understand the Bible in a way that is comforting and affirming *of the way we are and the way we live.* These idols need to be challenged. There are many, many biblical stories that do this very thing, for much of the Old and New Testament come at us from the perspective of the weak and the small — those people who do not have much going for them except their faith in God.

How can loving our neighbor be anything else than a "social issue"? We may not agree on how neighbors are to be helped. This is a complex and difficult issue. Since we are not wise enough, let us leave it to the experts! I suspect this is one of the most effective tools the devil uses to silence the prophets of our day. My friend, my reading of history reveals there are few "experts." It would seem that most of the "experts" have a greater problem than ignorance and that is the power of self-interest. Of course the office of prophet requires homework. It requires humility. The prophet Reinhold Neibuhr rightly reminded us that there is some "false prophet in all of us."

The English statesman, Oliver Cromwell, in warm debate with some of the religious people of his day, is reported to have said, "I beseech you by the bowels of Christ, consider the possibility that you maybe mistaken." This is a danger, but the greater danger is for Christians to hide behind their imperfections. The strength of our faith is not in being perfect, but in repentance and forgiveness.

Yes, there are risks. Most of us have grown up in an environment that is fearful of confrontations. In the church we have become especially sensitive to "hurting the feelings of others." Here the strong words of William Muehl of Yale need to be heard: "I resent the increasingly common effort to stifle debate on the ground that truth may embarrass those committed to error."

Prophet is a good word and a good office. It belongs to the

Jewish-Christian tradition. In that sense it belongs to us. It is a key word for us. We should not let it be lost, or even worse become trivialized. We are in good company. We are in the company of Jeremiah and Jesus.

One thing more: faithful prophets love their people. A faithful prophet in our time, Martin Luther King, Jr., said, "You won't change anybody whom you don't love." There is no question that both Jeremiah and Jesus loved their people. Listen to Jeremiah's anguish and love, revealed in these woe-filled words: "O that my head were waters, and my eyes a fountain of tears, that I might weep day and night for the slain of the daughter of my people." (9:1) These words ran with those of Jesus in his lament over Jerusalem when he cried, "O Jerusalem, Jerusalum, killing the prophets and stoning those who are sent to you! How often would I have gathered your children together as a hen gathers her brood under her wings, and you would not! Behold your house is forsaken." (vv. 34-35) In moving words we hear and feel Jesus' strong desire to save. Martin Luther, at a low and discouraging time in his life, preached a great sermon on the imagery of "the mother-hen and her chicks." He said, "When you look at the mother-hen and her chicks you see a picture of Christ and yourself better than any painter could paint . . . Behold, this is the loveliest mother-hen . . . But what happens? We refuse to be chicks . . . "[3]

Hearing again this lament of love and concern, we can better understand the reaction of those two people who walked with him on the way to Emmaus, calling him "Jesus of Nazareth, who was a prophet mighty in deed and word before God and all the people . . . " (24:19)

Yes, Jesus is more than a prophet. He is our Redeemer. But the message of redemption is set in the prophetic call to repentance. "Oh Jerusalem, Jerusalem . . . "

Amen

1. Durwood Buchheim, *Preaching Helps*, "Prophet, Pulpit, Pew and Politics!" (Chicago, Christ Seminary — Seminex).

2. William Barclay, *The Gospel of Luke*, (Edinburgh, The Saint Andrew Press, 1953), pp. 191-2.

3. Martin Luther, quoted from *Luther The Preacher*, Fred W. Meuser, (Minneapolis, Augsburg Publishing House, 1983), pp. 62-64.

The Mysterium Tremendum!

A student, evaluating another student's sermon, said, "You talked a lot about God, but I haven't the foggiest notion of what you mean by the word "God!"[1] There is honesty in that reaction, an honesty of which many of us are afraid. Yet it is healthier than the ever-popular, cozy familiarity with the Almighty — that kind of familiarity through which God becomes my buddy with whom I have groovy experiences. This is one reason there isn't much difference in our attitude when going to church, or to a movie, or to a lecture. We chit-chat before and after. We make small talk about the weather, vacations, and family. It is the "performance" which determines whether we got anything out of it or not. Anything mysterious going on here today? Hardly. And we leave with our evaluations. "Didn't get much out of it this morning." "Not much inspiration around here. The hymns were awful and the pastor obviously had a poor morning."

Isaiah's anguished cry arose in the presence of the High and Holy One: "Woe is me. For I am lost; for I am a person of unclean lips and I dwell in the midst of a people of unclean lips; for my eyes have seen the King, the Lord of hosts!" (6:5) This tormented cry is replaced by the modern, comfortable response, "Lord, I do the best I can. You know that. I can't do everything. You of all people understand that I am not perfect." Somewhere, I recall reading where C. S. Lewis called this sort of popular response to God a "flabby religion," and so it is.

But the other side of the coin is that many of us desire something more. Many of us are looking for something more substantial in our relationship with God than a relationship with someone whom we can manipulate, or bribe, just by putting in an appearance on

Sunday morning. Is there any way in which we can restore some healthy tension between the lowly "Lord who is our pal" and the High and Holy one who is our Lord?

I don't know.

But maybe the difficult and puzzling Transfiguration story might help us. For it is clear, in spite of the great mystery (or maybe because of it) that here the message is not one of coziness and comfortableness, but rather of transcendence and beyondness.

This is a difficult text. It describes a kind of religious happening most of us have never experienced. In Matthew's account, Jesus speaks of this experience as a vision. In Luke's version, Jesus tells us that this mysterious transfiguration change, came about only after much prayer. It is a strange episode, but it is not a stray one. It is written in the three Gospels and it is written in the same chronological place in the three Gospels. It is this place which marks the turning point in Jesus' ministry. Here he makes the decision to go to Jerusalem and predicts his suffering death. In the gospels of Matthew, Mark and Luke, this significant announcement is followed by the journey to the mountain where the Transfiguration takes place. We may be puzzled by this mysterious event, but the early church obviously thought it important.

Could it be that its great mystery is the reason for its importance? We, who do not like mysteries have to have an explanation for everything. We expect to figure everything out with our technology. Maybe this Transfiguration story is for us.

The story is rich in Old Testament imagery. It reminds us of Moses' awesome experience on Mount Sinai. We have the setting of the mountain, the voice, the cloud and the dazzling light. In addition, we have two strong Old Testament personalities in Moses and Elijah. These are two heroes of the faith, both of whom left this world under mysterious circumstances; both of whom talked with God from the mountains of Horeb and Sinai, and both of whom are mentioned in Malachi, the last book of the Old Testament. These powerful, emissaries of God now meet with the One whom Moses looked forward to, and for whom Elijah was regarded as the forerunner. They now meet with Jesus, the Christ. It has been suggested that the presence of Moses and Elijah confirm the Messianic mission of Jesus Christ. There seem to be overtones in that direction. But it is more than this. For the experience and the kind of majestic symbolism and language used to describe this experience — suggest a picture of God that is not going to be captured by a Poloroid camera, nor a God that sends warm fuzzies up and down our spine.

Back in 1917, in a book entitled the *Idea of the Holy,* Rudolph Otto attempted to describe this human encounter with God. He examined religion from the perspective of experience and feeling, rather than from that of intellectual content. He coined a phrase that describes this God-encounter — *"The Mysterium Tremendum."* The Transfiguration is a "mysterium tremendum" event. Here the majesty of God not only surrounds us, it engulfs us. It goes beyond our experiences. It exists apart from that which we can measure or taste or touch. Here is God beyond the boundary of everything we can figure out. The Transfiguration story is a strong Biblical witness to the otherness of God, to God the holy and invisible one, to God who is supernatural and transcendant.

While he was still speaking, a cloud appeared and covered them with its shadow and the disciples were afraid as that cloud came over them. (v. 34)

Humility, wonder, and fear are some of the proper responses before such a God. We can't know this God as we know, for example, what we had for breakfast or how we got to church this morning. But not only can this God not be explained or proven, neither can we dismiss him. Joseph Sittler rightly sees profundity in this experience and suggests that this is one of the reasons we confess Sunday after Sunday, "I *believe* in God, the Father Almighty, maker of heaven and earth." We don't *know* this God. We *believe in* this God.

In part of the Communion Liturgy, called the Canticle, we have these words:

Holy, holy, holy Lord, God of power and might:
Heaven and earth are full of your glory.
Hosanna, Hosanna, Hosanna in the highest.
Blessed it he who comes in the name of the Lord.
Hosanna in the highest. [2]

These are not ordinary words with most of us. Neither are they words upon which we can really get a handle easily, nor understand. Yet many times this moment of Communion is something special for me and I suspect similar experiences for many of you. I am saying that in some way, and somehow our routine, humdrum and anxious lives have been intersected, or brought into the focus of this God through these worship experiences. We need more than words. We also need symbols, music and time-honored traditions if we are to begin to experience the transcendant God revealed in Scripture.

For it is this theme of greatness and glory and holiness and mystery that is present in our text and in all of Scripture when the subject matter is God. The Psalmist responds, "In his hands are the depths of the earth; the heights of the mountains are also his, for he made it; his hands formed the dry land." (Psalm 95:4-5) The Evangelist Luke says it simply but profoundly in his famous Christmas text: "Glory to God in the highest heaven." (2:14) When such a God comes near, it is not the time for relaxation, but the time for awe and holy fear. Perhaps this wondering, adoring, fearing attitude is adequately encompassed in the word "praise." Here the moving words of the hymnwriter, W. Chalmers Smith, can help us:

> *Immortal, invisible, God only wise,*
> *In light inaccessible hid from our eyes*
> *Most blessed, most glorious, the Ancient of Days*
> *Almighty, victorious, thy great name we praise!*[3]

But we are not just to praise him. We are also to listen to him. For in this strange story a voice comes out of the cloud saying, "This is my Son, whom I have chosen — listen to him!" (v. 35) The terrifying presence of the Wholly Other has chosen to reveal himself in Jesus Christ! In Christ God has become visible and active on earth. The work of God takes place in this one person.

During the epiphany season, we were reminded of the infant Jesus who revealed the "Kings of Kings" and the lowly carpenter from Nazareth who revealed the Lamb of God. The text for this Sunday points us in the direction whereby Jesus is revealed in his true nature as divine being — the chosen one of God. Though he doesn't say a word throughout this entire experience, it is clear that he is the center of the stage. We have moved from Moses' mountain to Christ's mountain.

We are to listen to him! Paul describes him well in that majestic passage from his letter to the Colossians:

Christ is the visible likeness of the invisible God . . . For through him God created everything in heaven and on earth, the seen and the unseen things . . . Christ existed before all things . . . He is the head of his body the church; he is the source of the body's life. He is the first-born Son, who was raised from death, in order that he alone might have the first place in all things. For it was by God's own decision that the Son has in himself the full nature of God. Through the Son, then, God decided to bring the whole universe back to himself. God made peace through his Son's sacrificial death on the cross and so brought back to himself all things, both on earth and in heaven. (1:15-20)

We are to listen to *him* — not just to Jesus, the revolutionary, or Jesus, the Liberator; nor the popular Jesus of American piety, meek and mild, who blesses and forgives everything that we do. No, the Jesus we are to listen to is not "just my pal." He is *my Lord.* That is a much-needed message for our time. But there is also comfort and strength in this kind of message. Jesus is Christ and Lord. God has entered our world in him. God remains hidden. There is no way of making God obvious to anyone, nor is there any way of proving his reality. But the uniqueness of our faith is that it gives the mystery of God a name. God is the father of our Lord Jesus Christ!

In chapter four of the popular *Evangelical Catechism,* there are included a number of questions about God. These questions are introduced by these words: "We human beings are always trying to make sense out of our lives and world . . . We would like to understand the supreme or ultimate reality that exists behind everything . . . What is this reality?"[4]

These words represent a deep, spiritual hunger that is in our land. If they also describe you and your situation, I suggest that during the coming days of Lent, it won't be business as usual. Why not work your way through the Gospel of Luke? It is one way that we can listen to him.

Amen

1. Edmund E. Steimle, *God the Stranger,* (Philadelphia, Fortress Press, 1979), p. 45.
2. The Canticle "Holy, holy, holy Lord", p. 69, *Lutheran Book of Worship,* (Minneapolis, Augsburg Publishing House, 1978). Reprinted by Permission.
3. W. Chalmers Smith, *Lutheran Book of Worship,* "Immortal, Invisible," Hymn #526, (Minneapolis, Augsburg Publishing House, 1978). Reprinted by Permission.
4. *Evangelical Catechism,* (Minneapolis, Augsburg Publishing House, 1982).

Truth in the Inward Being

Let Us Pray: We confess that we are in bondage to sin and cannot free ourselves. We have sinned against you in thought, word, and deed, by what we have done and by what we have left undone. We have not loved you with our whole heart; we have not loved our neighbors as ourselves. Amen[1]

Do you think the Japanese were worse sinners because they lost the war? Do you think the Jews were worse sinners because six million lost their lives in the holocaust? Do you think Martin Luther King was assassinated because he was a worse sinner? Do you think . . . ?

So might read a modern version of the Gospel text that is in front of us today. It is not a comforting text. Rather, it challenges the arrogance of our complacent, self-righteous spirit and reminds us, along with the prophet Moses, "Do not come near; put off your shoes from your feet, for the place on which you are standing is holy ground." (Exodus 3:5)

The description of two public calamities (the kind TV would make much over today) shape the content of Jesus' direct and uncomfortable words. These disaster events which are only described in Luke's gospel brings to an end Jesus' conversations which began in chapter twelve. The tone of this ongoing dialogue is harsh. Jesus delivers a strong warning about the dangers of prosperity when in his judgment on the rich farmer, he says, "You fool, this very night your soul will be required of you." (12:20) Jesus calls his listeners hypocrites who can predict the weather, but are blind to what is going on in their lives and world. In our text this conversation is interrupted by the "news" that Pilate had his soldiers kill a group of

Galileans while they were worshiping in the Temple. It well could be that with this interruption went hope that Jesus would get off the subject. His words were hitting too close to home.

Whatever their motive, there is little question they hoped to link the Galilean tragedy with the popular belief that bad people had bad things done to them. The Galileans died tragically because of the way they lived. Bad things happen to bad people. This tit-for-tat understanding of life remains a popular belief. You get what you deserve and you deserve what you get. This kind of thinking is especially popular for those of us who have been spared a lot of suffering. It frees us from becoming too concerned about what happens to other people and proves that we are pretty good people. Nothing that bad has ever happened to us!

But Jesus has no time for this kind of thinking. He squashes the idea that the good get the good and the bad, the bad. He does so by giving an example of his own. "When the Tower of Siloam collapsed and eighteen were killed, do you think that they were worse offenders than all the others who dwelt in Jerusalem? I tell you, No; but unless you repent you will all likewise perish." (vv. 4-5) This answer does not mean that wrong doing carries with it no unfortunate consequences. We know that sin causes a great deal of personal unhappiness and suffering. But Jesus denies any kind of *automatic* connection between suffering and sin. Whether we die violently or peacefully offers no proof as to the kind of person we were.

In our text, Jesus is not as interested in the relationship between suffering and sin as he is in personal reform and conduct. Here the issue is repentance. The message is clear: *the repentant attitude is urgently required.* This issue is no quibble about trifles. Jesus' theme song throughout the Gospels is "repent for the Kingdom of heaven is at hand." When Jesus sent forth the twelve, it was not enough to cast out demons and heal the sick. They also preached that people should *repent!* Someone has discovered that, next to the resurrection, repentance is the most frequent theme in the Book of Acts. We know that in every important situation, repentance was the essence of Peter's preaching. In the life of Paul we have a powerful example of the repentant attitude.

But as we all know, repentance is not the "in" word today. Some years ago, I heard a great preacher, J. S. Whale, charge that our age has reinterpreted the New Testament theme of repentance. We have changed, "Repent, for the kingdom of heaven is at hand: to mean,

"Relax for the kingdom of heaven is at hand!" This "relaxed" attitude is reinforced by the discoveries of an interdisciplinary study of Christian beliefs and practices which were recently published in a book entitled *Faith and Ferment*. This study, based on the responses of more than 2,000 church members and pastors from all denominations in the state of Minnesota, is a close-up view of how faith affects life. The study revealed that 28% of the Christians interviewed believe humans are inherently good. This optimistic attitude is reflected in these words by one of those responding: "The day I die, I should only have to look up at my Maker and say, 'Take me,' Not, 'Forgive me.' I'm not saying that I am perfect . . . but I have led a life that I don't have to be ashamed of."[2]

It is hard to understand that kind of complacent attitude toward human nature, given the world we are living in:

- two destructive World Wars in addition to the Korean and Viet Nam conflict;
- the Holocaust and an unbelieveable escalation in violence and weapons;
- poverty and world hunger on the increase;
- booming sales in home security systems;
- growing numbers of people so fearful that they will not go out at night.

In the face of all this (and much more), it is difficult to understand that many churchgoing people do not see this life as being out of step with God. But maybe it is not so surprising. In the First Letter of John, we read, "If we say we have no sin, we deceive ourselves, and the truth is not in us." (1:8) Sin has never been a popular subject — especially *my* sin. I would like to suggest that the heart or essence of my sin and your sin is that of self-deception. As the New Testament makes clear, "We *do* deceive ourselves . . . " Perhaps the basic reason for being so vulnerable to deception is the great power of *self interest*. We tend to avoid questioning those areas of our lives that promote our own material well-being. Most of us love ourselves and our opinions more than we think. We play a lot of games in order to justify this great devotion to Me. We shape, explain, understand the circumstances of our life to serve our needs. We build convincing illusions that hide our deceptiveness. These illusions are so useful, and resorted to so much that we begin to accept them as reality. So we say, "Business is business and I am entitled to a fair profit;" "Don't look a gift horse in the mouth!"; "All is fair in love and war;" "That's politics;" "One has to survive;" "I'm a company person." So go our explanations and understandings. Self-deception becomes a way of coping with some of the tough ethical issues we face. But it is a false way of coping, it is an expedient way that prevents us from really seeing who we are and what we are really doing.

The "revolutionary" days in the early history of our country gives us a classic description of the great power of deception. "Enslavement" was the rallying cry of those leaders who wanted freedom from the "oppressive" English government. So Washington warned about the "shackles of slavery" and Adams called the English "our oppressors" and Jefferson spoke eloquently about the "plan for reducing us to slavery". Yet during all this, enslavement of the Blacks was legal in all thirteen colonies (Jefferson depended on slaves to run Monticello!). Such is the power of deception.

I am a teacher, called to a seminary to teach. In the formality and power of the "Call" I can ignore dozing and inattentive students and poor evaluations they may make of me. *What do they know?* I am the one who has the experience! My peers accept me. I am tenured! I must be a good teacher, otherwise I wouldn't be here! Such is the power of self-deception. In order to preserve my identity as a good teacher, I ignore all the signs to the contrary. The same process goes on, no matter who we are or what we do. Our practice of self deception is one of the reasons it is difficult to administer effective evaluation procedures. It is not only true with individuals. As noted above, deception is a highly-developed art in national diplomacy. This means that we are not only prone to be deceivers; we are also vulnerable to being deceived. This is one of the reasons politicians get elected and countries get into war.

In a useful book entitled *Truthfulness and Tragedy,* Stanley Hauerwas develops the uncomfortable thesis that ". . . the condition of self-deception becomes the rule, rather than the exception in our lives."[3] He uses Hitler's architect, Albert Speer and the Jewish Holocaust, to illustrate the tragic results of self-deception. Albert Speer became Hitler's right-hand person. He was an intelligent person who became a good architect. He grew up in a prosperous and professional family. He had a good childhood. He received a good education, fell in love, got married and seems to have been a loving husband and an attentive father. Yet his autobiography is one long confession of self-deception.

Here are some of Speer's reflections, taken from his book, *Inside the Third Reich*. Concerning his childhood, these words:

> *To this day I can feel the artificiality and discomfort of that world.*

As a young man with a bright future he said:

> *My position as Hitler's architect had soon become indispensable to me. Not yet thirty, I saw before me the most exciting prospects an architect can dream of . . . The ordinary party member was being taught that grand policy was much too complex for him to judge it.*

And this scary but understandable thought, which is repeated in so many different ways today:

> *I felt myself to be Hitler's architect. Political events did not concern me.*[4]

This book by Speer is a useful one for optimistic Christians to read and ponder. For it seems that every generation, no matter what its prior history, is vulnerable to having the wool pulled over its eyes. The penetrating and courageous words of Reinhold Niebuhr are instructive at this point: "Faith is always imperiled on the one side by despair and on the other side by optimism. Of these two enemies of faith, optimism is the more dangerous. Few people live in permanent despair."[5]

"Behold, thou desirest truth in the inward being." (Psalm 51:6) The Psalmist recognizes the great importance of this kind of honesty with self, but history and our own experiences are eloquent testimony as to its difficulty. In his chapter on self-deception, Dr. Hauerwas reminds us, "To be is to be rooted in self-deception. The moral task therefore involves a constant and courageous vigilance; to note those areas where the tendency has taken root."[6] John, in his epistle gives us similar advice in these memorable words: "If we confess our sins, he is faithful and just and will forgive our sins, cleanse us from all unrighteousness" (1:9). This is the point of this uncomfortable gospel. In both the Galilean or Siloam incident, Jesus does not judge either the righteousness or innocence of those caught in these events. One would expect some harsh words for Pilate and maybe the Galilean "Zealots" who were taking the law into their own hands and had gone too far. But instead, Jesus takes these events and turns them into examples — powerful examples of why people need to look at their own life and to get things straight. The parable of the barren fig tree is a continuation as well as accentuation of the warning, "except you repent . . . " Repentance is the reorientation of our life. It is recognizing the great power of the self-righteous spirit. It is accepting responsibility for deceptive actions. It is taking a good look at who we are and the direction we are going. It is "truth in the inward being." The season of Lent is a good time to nurture that truth.

Let us pray.

"For the sake of your Son, Jesus Christ, have mercy on us. Forgive us, receive us, and lead us, so that we may delight in your will and walk in your ways to the glory of your holy name. Amen[7]

1. *Lutheran Book of Worship*, "Brief Order For Confession and Forgiveness," (Minneapolis, Augsburg Publishing House, 1978), p. 56.

2. Joan D. Chittister, OSB & Martin E. Marty, *Faith and Ferment*, (Minneapolis and Collegeville, Augsburg Publishing House & The Liturgical Press, 1983), p. 88.

3. Stanley Hauerwas, *Truthfulness and Tragedy*, (Notre Dame, University of Notre Dame Press, 1977), pp 82-98.

4. Albert Speer, *Inside the Third Reich*, (New York, Avon Books, 1970), pp. 64 & 162.

5. Reinhold Niebuhr, *Beyond Tragedy*, (New York, Charles Scribner's Sons, 1937), p. 116.

6. Stanley Hauerwas, *Truthfulness and Tragedy*, (Notre Dame, University of Notre Dame Press, 1977), p. 95.

7. *Lutheran Book of Worship*, "Brief Order for Confession and Forgiveness," (Minneapolis, Augsburg Publishing House, 1978), p. 56.

What Do I Know About God?

A young man had recently been ordained. Shortly after this notable event, he dressed himself with loving care. There was the new, dark, grey suit, the color-coordinated clergy shirt and the well-polished shoes. As he looked at himself in the mirror, the effect was pleasing. Feeling good about himself, he walked out into the streets of his city. He found himself in a somewhat blighted section of town, hands in his pockets, wondering what to do next. All the time he was being watched by a drunk, who seemed unimpressed. Their eyes met and the drunk said, "Sonny, what do you know about God?" The young parson made no reply. He went back to his room, took off his clerical garb and pondered the question, "What do I know about God?"

The story is ancient and probably the victim of some embellishment, but the question it raises is genuine and timely. "What do I know about God?"

For me, the familiar and popular story of the Prodigal Son contains the best picture in all the Bible of what God is like. It is one of three parables (Luke 15), all of which dealing with the same concern. It is a concern for the lost — a lost coin, a lost sheep and a lost son. These stories came about because some of the respectable people of that time were quite critical of the bad company Jesus was keeping. Jesus, by eating with sinners, crossed the line that social custom had carefully drawn. Jesus said, "Rejoice with me." They said, "This man receives sinners." Their reaction points up the wisdom of the little girl who prayed, "God make all bad people good and all good people nice."

Jesus responds with a memorable story: A father who had two sons . . . " You remember the story. Remember how the younger son wanted to get away from the farm (and probably from his older brother)? His father, wanting a son and not a hired hand, let him go. For a while it probably went well for the young son, but the time came when he ran out of money and could no longer "fish in Bedigo Creek and drink the cold frosty ones!" He ended up on a farm feeding the hogs. Someone had said that it is a law of life, "that when we do as we please, we are seldom pleased with what we do." In any circle, but especially in Jewish circles, the pig pen is a powerful symbol of unfreedom. But it is here where this young person comes to his senses. I suspect it was the push of the hog yard as well as the pull of the father's house that created within him the spirit of repentance.

It makes for a very uncomfortable moment when we are finally honest with self and quit the game of pretending, but it is also a great moment. We are talking about a changed heart, a new direction: and that is what happened to this youngest son. And it looks like a genuine turnaround! There is no hint that he is going to take pride in the fact that he left home and go on TV and tell and retell how awful it was living with those hogs!

None of this. He heads for home and the stage is set for the shattering confrontation. There comes the unbelievable surprise of this story! We expect some kind of punishment. Instead we are told, "but while he was yet at a distance, his father saw him and had compassion, and ran and embraced him and kissed him." (v. 20) The word for "ran" is a technical one used for a footrace in a stadium. The father didn't just amble toward his son, he *raced* toward him. It's an unforgettable picture — racing down the road, robe lifted high so as not to stumble, so he can hug his wayward son. Love replaces dignity.

Some years ago, I received a "modern" understanding of this beautiful homecoming. It is in the form of a letter from a son to his father:[1]

Dear Dad:
I found your letter to me here on the desk.
Perhaps you didn't want me to read it, now that
I have come back home. But I'm glad I did. I
thank you for your patience — for your under-
standing and love — for your mercy and forgive-
ness. I thank you also for the wonderful
celebration on my return.

But Father—it was not the best robe clinging
about my starven frame;
Father — it was not the ring;
Nor yet the shoes, nor anything
Your kind, fleet-footed servant brought;
Father — 'twas the thought
That you, from your safe righteousness, could run
To your unworthy son.

Father — not the dancing nor the singing,
The feast, nor those who came,
Showed me your secret, and in part
Your long sight and your anguished heart.
Your friends and neighbors reverencing
Your ways, might marvel at the thing —
But I — my Father — I, your son,
A great way from you, saw you run.

Robe, ring, shoes — they are all powerful symbols of honor which indicate full and complete restoration to the family. There is no probationary period. There are no "I told-you-sos," no "I suppose-you-are-broke" responses. No, none of these joy-dampening words that most of us are so good at. Rather, the shocking, but wonderful announcement of a party with music, feasting and dancing. " 'For this my son was dead and is alive again; he was lost, and is found.' And they began to make merry." (v. 24)

So the town drunk who asked the young pastor, "What do you know about God?" raised a legitimate question. Here in the fifteenth chapter of Saint Luke's gospel we have Jesus' answer, God is like the shepherd who leaves the ninety-nine sheep and goes in search of the one who is lost. God is like the woman who loses a coin and searches diligently throughout the house until she finds it. God is like the father who runs out to meet and greet and hug his returning son who has wasted his life in riotous living. This is what God is like!

For me, this is the greatest picture in all Scripture. It is the beautiful picture of spontaneous, unconditional acceptance. To interpret this story in any other fashion would be to twist it. The wonder of it is that this *is* what God is like! Here is the answer to our question. God loves the unlovely ones, the unworthy ones.

This is the heart and center of what we believe. If we believe this story by Jesus Christ, we are saying that, behind and over and under our lives, there is a God who cares for us like the father in this story cared for his son. Before you go to sleep, or as you sit on the tractor, or wait for the school bus — think on this picture of the "father racing to his son to welcome him home." There is no better news than this.

But the story that gives us such a warm and moving picture of fun, laughter and joy, also gives us a graphic description of the opposite. For the story does not end with the celebration and the happy reunion. We remember this father had *two* sons, and our parable continues: "Now the elder son was in the field; and as he came and drew near to the house, he heard music and dancing . . . But he was angry and refused to go in." (vv. 25-28)

H. L. Mencken once defined Puritanism as "the haunting fear that someone, somewhere, may be happy." That same kind of joyless spirit seems to have been deeply ingrained in the elder Brother. Mark Twain is reported to have described the elder brother in this fashion: "A good man in the worst sense of the word." He lived in the same house. He worked next to his father for many years. Yet he is far removed from the spirit of joy and laughter. Parties and celebrations don't turn him on. They turn him off.

"Lo, these many years I have served you . . . " (v. 29)

These words tell us why. It was his impeccable "service" that prevented him from having a good time. It was hard for him to "unwind" because he was so busy "keeping score" to prove his dedication and responsibility. The "adding machine spirit," the spirit of always measuring and calculating, are big roadblocks to enjoyment. It seems that this kind of "measuring and judging" invariably leads to comparison, and that leads to condemnation. "All these years I have served you," translated means, "Someone isn't doing their share or someone isn't as responsible as I am. I am not appreciated around here!" Preachers are particularly vulnerable to the elder-brother spirit. "Year in and year out I have ministered to these people and for what? A miserly salary and some tomatoes and radishes when they are in season!" Or the long-time charter member: "What do these newcomers know about this congregation anyway? They should have been here when things were really tough."

When we can no longer see beyond the work we have done, then it is hard for us to appreciate love and joy and celebration. We can no longer enjoy parties because they are a waste of time and money. Something so frivolous has nothing to do with God and the church.

And we are right. But in our rightness we seem to shrivel and wither and become poor witnesses for the good news of Jesus Christ. There is so little joy in us. Maybe it is hard for us to be joyful *because it is hard for us to receive.* I don't know of a more popular word today, especially in church circles, than the word "Grace." But there seems to be precious little evidence of it. Maybe Karl Barth was right when he said, "Grace is always more devastating than judgment. Judgment is easy to take, but grace threatens the devil out of us!" Could that be why the opposite of joy is not sorrow, but unbelief? Laughter and joy, therefore, are some of the results of a trust in God our Father, who wraps his arms around us as he did the wayward son.

This is a serious issue. Our parable ends on a serious note. It ends with the younger son back in the arms of his family. But the older brother, with all of his dedication and hard work, also figures in. We would like to think he might come join the celebration, but the story does not have this kind of happy ending. It ends on a somber note that should impress us. The lost sheep was found and returned to the fold. The lost coin was found and put back into circulation. The prodigal returned and was accepted back into the father's house. The only failure in these moving parables of Jesus is that of the respectable, older brother. About him the story informs us, "He was angry and would not go in." No one shut him out. It seems that his own goodness created feelings of superiority which in turn made him into an unlovely kind of person. For these reasons I think this is an important story.

I am over sixty years old. At that age, I know the proverbial sand in the hour glass of time is running out. Although I am not losing a lot of sleep over it, I am concerned as to how I will handle these last years of my life. Will the elder brother spirit overtake me and make me essentially bitter, pessimistic and suspicious of happiness and parties? Or will I leave this world with people remembering an essentially positive spirit — one who in spite of growing infirmities could still enjoy life, people and parties?

This is not just an academic question. In the course of thirty years in the ministry I have been with many people as they moved toward the time of death. Some handled it well and some didn't. I remember old Joe who didn't handle it well. A whiner and complainer till the very end, he made life quite miserable for family and all who tried to minister to him. On the way back from the cemetery, Joe's neighbor told me not to worry about it because "Joe was born under a weeping willow." Is that the explanation?

There was Mildred. She was a widow for many years. During this time she was a cook in three different restaurants. She was also active in the woman's organization of her congregation. For a number of years she served as president. Then she suffered a debilitating stroke and had to be moved to the "Old Folk's Home." But even there, Mildred found meaning and purpose in living.

What makes the difference?

One has to be cautious about absolute answers, but this "difference" ought to be of vital interest to us, as we continue our pilgrimage, for we are on a journey home. But we are going home not to the arms of an elder brother, but the arms of our Father who runs out to meet us. "And he ran to his son . . . he said to his servants, bring quickly the best robe . . . we are going to have a party." (vv. 20-24) What a welcome! He was equally patient and kind to his disrespectful and uptight eldest son. "My son", the father answered, "You are always here with me and everything I have is yours." (v. 31)

This is what our God is like. May this picture of God become ever more meaningful and real for us, like the little girl who, in her Sunday bedtime prayers prayed, "God, I had a good time in church today. I wish you could have been there." May we, whatever our age, continue to have the time of our life, with this, the greatest story for any time.

Amen

---

1. The writer of this letter is unknown to the author.

Wasteful Love?

This is a strange story. "Anointing" is a ritual that is out of touch with most of our experiences. We are also suspicious of wasteful action, no matter what form it takes. We are practical people, and practical people have a hard time with extravagance. But this strange story is an important story. In one form or another it appears in all of the Gospels. The Gospel accounts do not agree in a number of details, yet all agree as to the "anointing," and all show indignation at the extravagant action of this woman whom John identifies as Mary. So the strange story is also a significant one. It is well for us to hear it.

It is the week of the Passover celebration. It is that time when around 100,000 faithful Jews come to Jerusalem to celebrate the great event in their history — remembering the time when the Angel of Death passed over their people. This is to be Jesus' final passover celebration. The hour of his death is near and no angel is going to save him. On his way to Jerusalem for the last time, Jesus arrives at the little town of Bethany. Here, he has a meal with old friends: Lazarus, whom he raised from the dead, and Mary and Martha, the sisters of Lazarus. Women have played an important role throughout the ministry of Jesus Christ, but as Crucifixion comes near so also grows their importance and visibility. It is likely this story would not have been remembered had it not involved Mary. She made this meal a memorable one, not by serving it, but by the warm, spontaneous act of her devotion.

Our text tells us that, during the course of the supper, "Mary took a pound of costly ointment and anointed the feet of Jesus and wiped his feet with her hair; and the house was filled with the fragrance of the ointment." (v. 3) This perfume was not of the dime-store variety; it was the genuine stuff, possibly made from the costly pistachio nut. We have further testimony to its high quality by the observation that "the house was filled with the perfume of the ointment?' Mary's extravagance brings an immediate response. In John's version of this story, it is Judas who pours on the cold water by asking the practical question, "Why was this ointment not sold for three hundred denarii and given to the poor?" (v. 5) Jesus, who was born poor and lived poor and died poor; Jesus, who believed his purpose was to "announce good news to the poor" (Luke 4:18); Jesus, who gave us the powerful, disturbing story of The Rich Man and Lazarus (Luke 16:19-32); Jesus, who defended, protected and cared for the Poor — this Jesus surprisingly takes Mary's side! In all four of the Gospel accounts of this story Jesus defends the act of this woman and, in all solemnity, blesses it. In our story he says, "Let her alone, let her keep it for the day of my burial. The poor you always have with you, but you do not always have me." (v. 7) In Mark's Gospel Jesus responds with these words: "Leave her alone; why do you trouble her? She has done a beautiful thing to me . . . She has done what she could; she has anointed my body beforehand for burying. And truly, I say to you, wherever the gospel is preached in the whole world, what she has done will be told in memory of her." (Mark 14:6-9)

Jesus was moved by this woman's unmeasured giving. There are not many things written in the New Testament that received this kind of praise. There was the soldier, the Centurion who showed a strong faith; another woman, the widow who put her whole living into the treasury; and now this woman, who anointed him with the costly perfume. He blesses her extravagant action and calls it beautiful. What she did has become a lasting memorial. As you have already heard, John tells us, "The house was filled with the perfume of the ointment." Some biblical interpreters see in these words the meaning that the whole church has been blessed by Mary's action.

But the story remains strange to our ears. We wonder, why was it preserved in all the gospels? Why is it important? What is its point? Part of the story's importance is that it points to Jesus' death. Mary's action calls attention to the coming death and burial of Jesus. This anointing happened during the Passover celebration — a festival calling to mind and heart that time in history when God intervened and death was passed over for the people of Israel. In its timing (before the Crucifixion), in its setting (the Passover Festival), and in the "anointing," we are being reminded that Jesus' death is not just an ordinary execution. Jesus' anointing is pointing us to the great truth that his coming death was a sacrificial one and effecting the new deliverance for the people of God.

But it seems clear that the main importance of this story centers in Mary's extravagant action. It was this action that was challenged by Judas as being wasteful. That point we understand! Mary's action was irresponsible from our point of view. For a few minutes the room was filled with the sweet aroma, but then it was gone with the evening breeze. It disappeared into nothingness. All that remained of the equivalent of something like $60.00 in our currency was an empty bottle. We too are puzzled, maybe even offended, by Jesus' praise. Or maybe we handle his commendation of Mary like we handle some other things he said or did with which we don't agree. "What do you expect? After all, he was the Messiah. You would *expect* him to act in that fashion. But we all know you can't run the world that way! We have to be practical."

Here is the point of this story. It brings out into the open the tension between action based on common-sense predicted results and those that seem to be done for no reason but love — foolish love at that! Here is the main reason this story is so strange to us! It seems far removed from the spirit of our day, a spirit which needs to know the bottom line of everything before we risk anything. Our Lord ignores the practical objections and praises this foolish action of love: not toward a needy neighbor; not toward an endowment fund, whose interest can be used forever; but an impulsive, spontaneous act of devotion that was directed solely to him.

In the delightful book, *Zorba the Greek,* the main character is certainly no Mary, but there are striking similarities. Zorba is impulsive, spontaneous and irresponsible, but at the same time he is warm and loving. Zorba's uptight boss is envious of Zorba's attitude, but he can't break the tight string of respectability and responsibility. Zorba describes him in this fashion:

> A man's head is like a grocer; it keeps accounts. I've paid so much and earned so much and that means a profit of this much or a loss of this much. The head's a careful little shopkeeper; it never risks all it has, always keeps something in reserve. It never breaks the string.

And the boss responds:

All that Zorba said was true. As a child I had been full of mad impulses, superhuman desires, I was not content with the world. Gradually, as time went by, I grew calmer, I set limits, separated the possible from the impossible, the human from the divine, I held my kite tightly, so that it should not escape."[1]

Like the responsible "boss" in this story, we are attracted, yet embarrassed, by this sort of uncontrolled life. "It's exhibitionist! Such things simply aren't done in our circles. Surely God sees through that kind of foolishness." So we sit on our emotions and no one is going to get a "hallelujah" out of us (not even in our closet) no matter how hard we are squeezed.

The mother asked her little daughter what she was praying for. She responded, "I wasn't praying for anything, I was just loving God." We men may think this kind of devotion is for the women and all of us who are older may think it is only for the little ones. But Jesus liked it! We remember the ancient command about "loving God with all our heart, soul and mind." That doesn't leave much out, does it? We know we don't have to love God because he commands it, but rather in grateful response to his creative and accepting love. He created us, in his image. We belong to him. We would not be here, nor would we be who we are, without God. The warmth and greatness of this love was seen already in the call to Israel: "Fear not, for I have redeemed you; I have called you by name, you are mine." (Isaiah 43:1) And from the New Testament we hear it in the familiar and moving promise, "God so loved the world that he gave his only Son . . . that we might have eternal life." (John 3:16) About this God, the honored Swiss theologian Karl Barth said, "His love is the burning fire which cannot be quenched." Does it not warm our hearts? In its warmth and power can we not drop our emotional guard a bit and praise him in our prayers? Maybe thank him as we clean the oven or plow the field or make our sick calls? Or maybe even here in this place we could surprise ourselves (and our neighbor?) and love God in "letting go" in the joyful songs and "noise" when we sing. Can we laid-back, bottom line, Christians not loosen up a bit in loving God?

Remember, Jesus wasn't embarrassed or offended by it. He liked it. He called it beautiful — and probably not just because he was the recipient, but also because of Mary's reckless extravagance. Paul Tillich described Mary's action as "holy waste, that is waste growing out of the abundance of Christ.'' He reminds ''that we are sick not only because we have not received love, but also because we are not allowed to give love, yes allowed to waste themselves.[3] We know that! We don't like living where everything is measured and planned and calculated because it becomes dull and routine and boring. Yet we are afraid to really believe it, or live that way.

A good friend of mine told this delightful, personal story. It is a true story and it happened in the recent days of the Seminary Fund Appeal [in the American Lutheran Church]. My friend, a person of modest means, was visited by a Seminary colleague of mine for a possible gift. After the proper information had been shared, my friend was asked if he might not consider a gift of $10,000.00. That kind of gift request was totally unexpected. It was out of sight, out of mind and out of everything else! But this good, polite couple talked it over and agreed that over a five-year period they could do it. They said yes! In hearing the story, I didn't hear any pride. I did not hear any self-righteousness. But I did hear surprise. I did hear satisfaction and I did hear great joy. Their impulsive, reckless, irresponsible response may not be filling the church with the aroma of its sweet smelling perfume, but I sense their lives have been filled with great satisfaction and joy.

Could it be that when it comes to love, there isn't such a thing as waste?

Amen

1. Nikos Kazantzakis, *Zorba the Greek,* (New York, Ballantine Books, 1964), pp. 334-35. Reprinted by permission.

2. Karl Barth, *Church Dogmatics, the Doctrine of Reconciliation,* (Vol. IV), (Edinburgh, T & T Clark, 1958), p. 767.

3. Paul Tillich, *The New Being.*

Thinking About the Church

Recently I heard this definition of the church: "The church is that place where the person you least want to live with always lives. And when that person moves away, someone else arrives to take his or her place." Thomas Paine said, "My mind is the church." Thomas Jefferson said, "I am a sect myself." The story goes that when Mr. Jefferson heard he would not go to heaven except with a group, he announced that he would not go at all!

There are a growing number of people today who say, "I like Jesus, but I don't like his church." What do you think about that statement? What do you think about the church? Is the church necessary for our salvation? If the church speaks, how important is it that we listen? What makes a church successful? What is the purpose of the church? When you think about the church, what do you think about?

Here is how one person answered that question: "I go to church to be with good people, to be with my friends?" Here is another: "I go to church so I can make it through the week." Here the church is something like a hospital or garage where we can get a weekly, personal tuneup. Or consider this picture of the church: "I don't go to church because I don't know which is the right one?" Or: "I don't go to church because no one is going to tell me how to live?" Personal sanctification, that's the mission of the church and this person wants nothing to do with it. When we think about the church, what do we think about?

Our Lenten journey is coming to a close. Holy Week is near at hand. Many of us have made this journey before. We know what is ahead. We know the tragedy that is coming. The Gospel before us this morning helps us to understand this tragedy.

The story comes about because some good people did not like Jesus. They didn't like him because he was causing them problems with people who did like him. So they raised the question of credentials or authority. This is an age-old tactic which remains quite popular in our time. Don't get trapped into discussing the real issues, just keep on raising questions. Don't deal with the content of the teaching, rather focus on the teacher. Is the teacher one of us? Does the teacher understand our problems? Of course, beneath the questions lies the *real* question, "Who controls the teacher?" As we know, Jesus faced these questions before. He didn't answer them then and he doesn't now. His style is to respond with a story.

His story is about an absentee landlord who had rent-collecting problems. After a long time, with no return from the vineyard, the owner sends a servant to collect. The servant is beaten and sent away empty handed. The landlord sends two more messengers but all return empty handed, each being treated more severely than the previous one. At this point, one would think more drastic, forceful action would be called for. But instead of the sheriff, the owner sends his son. Yet when the last messenger arrives and is identified, the tenants say to themselves, "This is the heir. Let us kill him, that the inheritance may be ours." (v. 14)

It isn't difficult to make the proper connections because this story reads more like an allegory than a parable. God is the owner of the vineyard. Israel is the vineyard. The tenants of this vineyard are the religious leaders of Israel. The messengers were the prophets of the Old Testament. The son of the owner is Jesus Christ. His murder is his crucifixion as the Son of God.

In the book of Isaiah (5:1-7) there is the moving story that begins with these words, "My friend had a vineyard." The prophet goes on to tell us that it was a good vineyard, well situated on a sunny, fertile hill. The vineyard was not only well located, but was given every attention. The soil was carefully cultivated and the tedious task of stone removal was thoroughly done. Imagine, then, the owner's keen disappointment when, instead of beautiful grapes, he found only wild grapes. Jesus, as well as his audience, may have been familiar with this powerful Old Testament story.

So this story became a continued but condensed version of the history of salvation. The lesson of the stories is this: Judgment comes upon the people of God because they forgot to whom the vineyard belonged. Like too many people before and since, they acted as though they owned the vineyard and therefore controlled it. This kind of arrogance is demonstrated in their rejection and murder of the Son. This rejection of Christ was the decisive element. "Everyone who falls on that stone will be broken to pieces; but when it falls on anyone it will crush him." (v. 18) This verse, which is found only in Luke's gospel is found in other Jewish writings in these words: "Should the stone fall on the crock, woe to the crock. Should the crock fall on stone, woe to the crock. In either case, woe to the crock?" (p. 189, Talbert)

The point of the story is clear. Our response to Jesus Christ is the main criterion by which our churches are judged. Luke, early in his gospel, issued this warning in the words of Simeon to Mary, the mother of Jesus: "Behold, this child is set for the fall and the rising of many in Israel." (v. 2:34) In the Book of Acts, the old refrain sounds in these words: "This is the stone which was rejected by you builders, but which has become the head of the corner. And there is salvation in no one else, for there is no other name under heaven given among men by which we must be saved." (Acts 4:11-12) The focus is on Jesus Christ. Response to him determines one's destiny.

Now back to this vineyard and our thinking about it. If we believe God is the owner/controller of this vineyard, that should help us in our thinking, shouldn't it? For example, it is hard to imagine God as the owner/controller of a "club" or "business" where we are the "members" or "customers" and the pastor is the executive director! But if we go to church to "feel good" or to be affirmed in our style of living, aren't we in danger of making it into something it shouldn't be?

Furthermore, if God is the owner/controller of this vineyard, do we not have to be concerned about the kind of crop that is being harvested? When the messenger comes around for the rent, can we tell him that we have used up the crop in feeding ourselves?

Some years ago I read this description of some of our vineyards: "And men clubs gathered in order to gather and the parish was happy that one-hundred men had turned out to eat and listen to a secular address. And some women's groups met in order to raise money in order to meet the budget in order that they might have a place to meet to raise money to reach the budget . . . " There are a growing number of people who are unhappy with the church. Could this be the reason, that too many churches live for themselves?

Well, if the church isn't a "club" or a "business," just what *is* it? One suggestion I heard — and liked is this: "The church is a 'halfway house.' " Halfway houses help people get back into society, not to escape from society. They are not for "nice" people, but for broken, sinful people who need the help and acceptance and community of a halfway house. But because of this, there is no perfect harmony in halfway houses. Neither do halfway houses have the reputation of being fragile, or tame or domesticated or places that are afraid of conflict. They actually help sinful people get back into a sinful world. Halfway houses are willing to take chances on people. So, how about changing the name of the vineyard to, "Saint Luke's Lutheran [Methodist, Roman Catholic] Church — Halfway House of the Lord!"

But maybe that's too bold so how about calling our churches, "Workshops of the Holy Spirit"? Workshops have the smell of action and activity about them. Something is going on in workshops. People are not just sitting around complaining that the pastor doesn't inspire them! Rather they are about the business of "building up the body of Christ" (Ephesians 4:11-12), and that kind of perspiration brings with it a lot of inspiration!

We are thinking about the church, which means thinking about this particular vineyard of which we are the tenants. Do we see this vineyard as a place of comfort or challenge? Are we more concerned about meeting our own needs than the needs of others? Do we look like a church but smell like a museum? Would Christ have remained alive in our hearts, had it not been for this particular vineyard?

These are not comforting questions, but they are useful questions for us tenants to ponder as we move into Holy Week and the suffering and crucifixion of the One who is the owner/controller of this vineyard. In his letter to the friends of the runaway slave, Philemon, the Apostle Paul makes this beautiful request: "Refresh my heart in Christ." (Philemon v. 20) Could that be where we ought to begin again? Let's focus not on some name-changing program or self-study process; not in pointing the finger at the leadership of this vineyard or the wicked times in which we live, but rather let us stay with the issue of your stewardship and mine — in this vineyard. The Lord of the vineyard is faithful. His promise remains, "I am the vine, you are the branches. Whoever remains in me and I in you will bear much fruit for you can do nothing without me. You did not choose me but I chose you and appointed you to go and bear much fruit, the kind of fruit that will endure.'' (John 15:1-17)

O Lord, let us not become weary in well doing. Refresh our hearts so that with passion and enthusiasm we might be good stewards in your vineyard.
Amen

Courtroom or Home?

There is an ancient story about Moses that goes something like this:

> *A beggar once came to Moses and asked him for bread. "Come into my tent," said Moses, "and you shall eat with me." The beggar entered the tent and Moses set out food for both of them. Before eating, Moses gave praises to God. Not so the beggar, who watched in silence while Moses gave thanks. "Why do you not praise God?" asked Moses. "Why should I praise God?" asked the beggar, "What has he done for me? Why has he allowed me to be so poor?" Hearing these words, Moses became very angry. He picked up his staff, beat the beggar and drove him from his tent without any food. When the beggar had gone . . . so the ancient story runs . . . God came to Moses and said, "Moses, why did you not feed the beggar and why did you beat him?" "Because he would not praise you, Lord," said Moses, feeling very righteous. "Moses," said God, "that man has not praised me for twenty years and he is still alive. He has not praised me because all that time you have neglected him. He is only alive at all because I am less religious than you are, and have not suffered him to perish. It seems to me, Moses, that if I were as religious as you appear to be, there would be no one left on the earth."*[1]

This mythical story points up an uncomfortable truth church members have a convenient way of forgetting. Many years ago a famous preacher preached on the theme "Sinners in the hands of an angry God." Concerning this theme, the thought was expressed by one person who said he would rather be in the hands of an angry God than in the hands of his Christian neighbor next door! We who have been around the church awhile know that religion doesn't automatically bless a person with the spirit of charity. In this connection, Reinhold Niebuhr shares this uncomfortable but on-target observation. "If there were a drunken orgy somewhere, I would bet ten to one a church member would not be in it. But if there were a lynching, I would bet ten to one that a church member was in it."[2] It was this theologian who also said, "Not much evil is done by evil men. Most evil is done by good people who do not know that they are not good." It is to these uncomfortable truths that our text speaks.

Those of you who are familar with this story know that there is some question as to its validity. This cloud of suspicion is indicated in the Revised Version of Scripture, for there this story appears in a footnote. The reason for this is that this story is not found in the majority of old manuscripts. I will not bother you with the technical arguments concerning the story's genuineness. It is the opinion of many biblical scholars that it is too life-like to be fictitious. As has been pointed out, "it is most unlikely that the Church even invited this incident. She may have been embarrassed by it, but once having heard it she could never forget it." I share the opinion of the Johannine scholar, Raymond Brown, who wrote, "The delicate balance between the justice of Jesus in not condoning the sin and his mercy in forgiving the sinner is one of the great gospel lessons."[3]

This exquisite drama probably happened during that period in Jesus' ministry when his popularity with the ordinary people had intensified the hatred of the Scribes and Pharisees. They wait for the chance to get even. This opportunity comes through this woman who was caught in the act of breaking the Sixth Commandment (concerning adultery). They bring this woman before Jesus and, with pious unction, cite the law of Moses. The law is clear. The transgressor must be punished by stoning. Jesus is faced with the question, "What do you say about her?"

These, good, religious people, who were placing Jesus in this predicament, apparently felt more comfortable in the *courtroom*. Their world was governed by precise laws. It was a world of right and wrong, a world where respectability is all-important and where respectability is measured by appearances. They measured things by what you would say and do and not by what you might think or feel. It makes for a tidy kind of world, because in it you have only two kinds of people — bad and good.

This woman committed the terrible crime of adultery. There was no question about that. This meant she must be stoned. If you live in the courtroom, the answers are generally simple and uncomplicated. But notice, please: there is a kind of hardness that goes with this kind of living. We can sense this harsh, unfeeling attitude in this story. This woman meant nothing to them. She was a thing, not a person. Unfortunately our history is full of such examples. We men ought to be angry as well as penitent at how society has treated women and how slow, *so very slow,* we were to recognize this bondage of women. I think of my own mother. I am sure she loved my father and he loved her, but there was no question about who had the better of it. Life on the farm was no picnic for either, but it was terribly, terribly hard for the woman. We males just took that kind of hardship and sacrifice for granted. That was the woman's lot. In the whole area of sexual relationships, it is still the woman who carries most of the responsibility. It takes two to commit adultery, but in our story no mention is made of the man. The woman — *she* was looked upon as a pawn in the men's game to destroy Jesus. They are taking advantage of her guilt to further their own evil designs. Through her they hope to pin Jesus on the horns of a dilemma. (Not unlike that time when some of them gave him a Roman coin and the question, "Should we pay taxes to Caesar or not?"). They are not really interested in *people.* They are interested in *hurting,* and *winning* and *embarrassing* and *proving their own rightness.* If Jesus said, "let the woman die," he would be untrue to many of the little people who had trusted him and he would certainly be in trouble with the Roman authorities. On the other hand, if he said, "Let the woman go," they could accuse him of breaking the law of Moses. I imagine that it is with inward delight they sneak up on Jesus, saying, "According to the law, Moses commanded us to stone such women — now what do *you* say about her?" '

How would we answer their question? More to the point, how *do* we answer? Would we be the first to pick up a stone? This might be too brutal for our soft hearts. It might be more to our taste to give this woman a stern lecture on the consequences of the sins of the flesh. Or perhaps we would rush to the nearest phone, so that we might share her sad predicament with all our friends. Aren't we cruel and malicious at times? Doesn't the urge to get even become so strong that it causes us to run roughshod over the feelings of people? Why else do we take such inward delight in the misfortunes of other people? How else do we explain our tendency to make like lawyers cross-examining the motives and actions of people with whom we don't agree, or whom we don't like?

I am continually amazed at how much time we all spend in taking other people apart, and how little time we spend taking ourselves apart. One wonders whatever happened to the meaning of that commandment we learned in confirmation, about "putting the most charitable construction on what other people do"? The Apostle Paul reminds us, "Brethren, if a person be overtaken in a fault, ye who are spiritual restore such a one in the spirit of meekness, lest thou also be tempted." (Galatians 6:1) In the spirit of meekness — is that the way we attempt to put people back together?

In the courtroom of life, the spirit of meekness is usually absent. It is replaced by a kind of pride which permits our own weaknesses to blind us, and our hunger for self-justification urges us to make others look worse than we are. Is this where we live? Do we see our role in life as that of a prosecuting attorney? Or as a member of the family? Dr. Paul Tournier, the Swiss Psychiatrist, sees the woman in our story as "symbolizing all the despised people of the world . . . all those people who we see daily crushed by just and unjust judgments. And her accusers symbolize the whole of judging, condemnatory contemptuous humanity."[4] The question remains: where are *we*?

The good people of Jesus' day are waiting for an answer. They continue to press Jesus for his. When they see him hanging his head, tracing figures on the ground, they are sure they have him where they want him. Are they perhaps so used to hating and bitterness that they no longer see other possibilities? Maybe they are so used to seeing nothing but evil in other people, so used to rejoicing over the troubles of other people, that they no longer can feel sympathy. Could it be that Jesus is so embarrassed by the viciousness of their deed and so full of sympathy for the woman being judged, that he has to look away? But they will not let him alone. Again comes the question, "What shall we do with this woman?" Finally Jesus stands erect and they have their answer, "He that is without sin among you, let him cast the first stone." (vv. 7-8) And so the accusers fall into the pit that they have dug with their own judgments. "Judge not that you may not be judged," Jesus preached to us on the Sermon on the Mountain. (Matthew 7:1) The proverbial saying of the world puts it even more succinctly: "If you choose to fight with the tomahawk, you should expect someday to receive a scalping."

This answer by Jesus is not just a clever response or a slick evasion of the issue. Neither is Jesus here undermining the administration of the law. He is not requiring guiltlessness before one can punish evildoers. Such an attitude would wreck any social order. But here Jesus is dealing with zealots for the word of the Law, but they are not interested in the spirit. Had these religious leaders brought this woman before the ordinary courts, it would have been a different matter. But crawling into God's domain under the pretensions of holiness and asking about the punishment of adultery, they get Jesus' answer: "Let him who is without sin cast the first stone." In other words, God's kingdom is not a courtroom. It is instead a home. It is the place where we consider the plank in our own eye before we start searching for the splinter in our brother's eye." (Matthew 7:3-5)

In God's kingdom there are not two labels, the bad and the good. In his kingdom there are not two human distinctions, the guilty and the righteous. In his kingdom, there are only the guilty. "If thou, Lord, should mark iniquities, O Lord, who shall stand?" (Psalm 130:3) The Psalmist's question remains ever timely and pertinent. All humanity is bankrupt in reference to goodness. In this story Jesus is telling us that we all live in glass houses! If that is the case it is well for us to keep our hands away from the stone pile. In God's kingdom it is not only the bad people who are sinful, but good people too. Years ago, Emil Brunner said, "A sinner is not a human being who has sinned a certain number of times, he is a human being who sins in whatever he is doing." Professor C. S. Lewis has pointed out that if a tiny baby had the strength of a full grown person, this person would be the most terrifying creature on earth. "No one is born prejudiced in favor of others, but everyone is born prejudiced in favor of one's self." Good people, especially religious people, have a tendency to ignore this disturbing truth. When we do, we are headed for the courtroom and not the home.

Jesus, having given his answer, silence now comes over this uncomfortable gathering. We can scarcely imagine what was going on in the heart of this woman at this moment. Was she bracing herself for the first stone? It did not come. No one was willing to throw the first stone. We can imagine the accusers edging their way out through the crowd. With the sudden turn of events, they want nothing more to do with the nasty business. With characteristic bluntness, Martin Luther describes their exit in this fashion: "They can look no one in the face, but must turn tail and sneak out of the Temple, slinking out as a dog with a burned snout slinks from the kitchen."[5]

Jesus is left alone with the woman. Will he now preach to her? Will he leave her, ignore her? He does none of the above. The woman is no longer in the courtroom. She is in a home. She is no longer facing the battery of prosecuting attorneys, but the Son of the Heavenly Father, who came to seek and save the lost and forgotten ones. "Woman, did no man condemn you?" And she said, "No one, Lord." And Jesus said, "Neither do I condemn you. Go, and sin no more." (vv. 10-11)

It has been pointed out that, technically, this is no declaration of forgiveness from Christ because we see no signs of repentance on the part of the woman. Technically this may be correct, but common sense tells me that Jesus' words, "Neither do I condemn you" are the words of absolution. Our Lord is not making light of her sin. He does not deny her guilt. He blots it out. "Go and sin no more" is recognition of the sin and "neither do I condemn you" is his pronouncement of forgiveness. Not only is there mercy here, but there is sensitivity and beauty in how our Lord bestowed it.

We do not know what became of this woman. We hear nothing more about her. But don't we have the right to believe that she left Jesus with hope alive in her heart? She discovered that she was not always to be regarded as the defendant. Jesus looked upon her as a member of God's family. She learned that she did not have to spend her life in the courtroom, but, because of Jesus, God welcomed her into his home.

Where do *we* live? Truthfully, aren't we found in both places — the courtroom *and* the home? Are we not *all* accused and accusers, both on trial *and* a trial *to* someone, the persecuted *and* the persecutor? The kingdom is not a law court and we are not God's prosecuting attorneys; but still we must confess with Paul, "I do not do the good I want, but the evil I do not want is what I do." (Romans 7:19) Even as God's children we live in a world of judging and being judged. To quote Luther again, "Let the stones lie. I will not pick any either. Let them lie, and do not throw at one another. Drop the stones, and say, 'Forgive our debts, as we have forgiven our debtors.'[6] Here too we continue to experience both our guilt and his grace. With the woman of our text and with all forgiven sinners of all ages we can rejoice and praise God in the words of Paul: "There is therefore now no condemnation to them which are in Christ Jesus." And again, these great words from the Apostle: "Who shall say anything to the charge of God's elect? It is God that justifies. Who is he that condemns? It is Christ that died, yes rather that is risen again, who is even at the right hand of God, who also makes intercession for us." (Romans 8) But let us remember, this only holds true for us as we feel our need for it. It is important to remember that to the frightened woman he said, "Go and sin no more," while to the righteous and respected ones, he said, "Let him who is without sin cast the first stone." Grace is for people trembling in their own guilt. Jesus said, "I did not come to call the righteous, but sinners." (Matthew 9:13)

Amen

1. The source of this story is unknown to the author.

2. Reinhold Niebuhr, quoted in *Courage to Change,* June Bingham, (New York, Charles Scribners Sons, 1961), p. 147.

3. Raymond E. Brown, *The Gospel According to John I-XXI,* (New York, Doubleday and Company, Inc., 1966), p. 337.

4. Paul Tournier, *Guilt and Grace* (New York, Harper & Brothers, 1962), p. 111.

5. Martin Luther, *Luther's Works,* Vol. 23, (St. Louis, Concordia Publishing House, 1959), p. 314.

6. *Ibid.,* p. 314.

The Power of Darkness

"But this is your hour, and the power of darkness." (v. 53) With these words, Jesus surrenders to the chief priest and the temple guard. These words not only usher in, they also set the tone for, the violent storm of madness that is about to engulf him. Crowds which had acclaimed him with their hosannas will soon be shouting, "Crucify! Crucify!" A short while ago he had been hailed as the conquering king but now he is on his way to a God-forsaken death. Jesus introduces this violent, bewildering, contradicting concoction of events with the somber appraisal: "But this is your hour, and the power of darkness." John in his gospel makes the same assessment in these words: "And this is the judgment, that the light has come into the world and men loved darkness rather than light, because their deeds were evil." (John 3:19)

Recently I finished reading a book entitled, *The Nazi Seizure of Power*. It is a disturbing book, describing how an average, middle class, predominantly Lutheran town of Northeim, joined the Nazi movement. This book is the result of a doctoral dissertation by William Sheridan Allen, who through reports, records and interviews studied the daily life experiences of this Lutheran Christian community. It is a chilling book because it details how a civilized, democratic, Christian community can be enveloped by darkness. This town of 10,000 citizens was 86 percent Lutheran. But it was also a divided town. The "poor" of the town wanted better treatment and so favored the movement of Socialism. The middle class was satisfied with the way things were and so wanted the political "Left" removed. The Nazis were able to exploit this division with the blessing and support of the Lutheran Church and its pastors.

It was also a town with a strong commitment to nationalism and militarism. The people of Northeim liked parades and watching soldiers march. In the book we read these words by Hitler: "Cruelty impresses, cruelty and raw force. The simple man in the street is impressed only by brutal force and ruthlessness. Terror is the most effective political means."[1]

The attitude of bitterness grew with growing poverty, terror and a sense of futility. This spirit of bitterness encouraged solutions through violence. From a quiet, orderly town, Northeim became a center of violence. Ultimately the struggle centered in two groups, between which there was no middle ground. Each to the other had become the evil enemy to be destroyed. One party wanted to institute a dictatorship; the other wanted to save the battered democracy.

In three short years, the Nazis, who in the beginning posed as devout Christians, gained control of the town. Once they were in power, they showed their true colors. But then it was too late. Such is the power of darkness. "For we are not contending against flesh and blood but against the principalities, against the powers, against the world rulers of this present darkness, against the spiritual hosts of wickedness in the heavenly place." (Ephesians 6:12)

Today we are at Calvary. The Church is also there, represented by Caiphas and his followers. They are devout people of good will. They have the best interests of their community at heart. They are orthodox, conservative believers. They spent their lives waiting for the Messiah. From these pious defenders of the faith we would expect support and sympathy for this Christ who is being humiliated. But in their darkness, these people of good will cry, "Crucify him! Crucifiy him!"

The government, represented by Pilate and Herod is also there. They stand for a government that has a good reputation for upholding the main tenants of law and order. Surely they will not permit any "lynch mentality" or "frontier justice" to operate in their jurisdiction! But the record reads that "Herod and Pilate became friends," (v. 12) and, "Jesus, Pilate delivered up to their will." (v. 25) "The mantle of greatness had been handed to the prefect of mighty Rome, but he would have been better off never to have tried it on for size. Attempting to go down quietly in history as a clever administrator he ended up embalmed in the Apostle's Creed."[2] Such is the power of darkness.

The common people are there. Surely these ordinary ones, with no particular or personal "stones to grind," surely they will be equal to the test. Surely they will link arms and unite against the oppresive Church and government and march in solidarity, chanting, "Release Jesus! Release Jesus!" But the record is clear and we read, "But they were urgent, demanding with loud cries that he should be crucified. And their voices prevailed." (v. 23)

"And their voices prevailed." The old appeal for public order and social stability can and has covered a multitude of devious deeds. Northeim, Germany is just one example among many. Such is the *power* of darkness. This subtle power of evil is and remains one of the great and needed lessons of the cross of Jesus Christ. We are reminded that those responsible for the crucifixion of Jesus were not the riff raff of society. It wasn't the dope addict, or the prostitute, or the mother on welfare who put Jesus on the cross. So called "bad" people have no monoply on the power of darkness. The Cross of Christ demonstrates clearly that which history also proves — that the perverse wickedness and injustices of history are predominately the work of good people.

Today we are at Calvary. Now *we* are the ones under scrutiny. Darkness is upon us when we refuse to see the sin that is in us. To "walk in darkness" is to lie to ourselves and the truth is not in us. (1 John 1:6) But why is the darkness so attractive. What makes us vulnerable to its demonic power? Self at any cost? Isn't that the essence of this darkness? Isn't that the reason it is so easy for us to favor solutions to the problems that are caused by other people? We are hardly ever the problem! We get angry over such terrible sins as not going to church, or not praying, or not reading the Bible. We decry homosexuality, or welfare cheaters while the sins of greed, selfishness and hate go unchallenged. Jesus described this kind of "darkness" as "swatting at gnats while swallowing camels."

I have spent nearly thirty years as an ordained minister in the church. I have yet to hear any persistent or telling criticism of how much I eat, drink or wear, even though a third of our world is starving. Yet throughout my ministry I have heard the criticism that our seminaries are no longer teaching the Bible and too many of our pastors no longer believe in the Virgin Birth or the Resurrection of Jesus Christ. We have devisive and energy-draining debates over doctrine but little attention is given to Christian service. Such is the power of the darkness revealed at Calvary. It warps and twists our priorities.

In a *New Yorker* magazine cartoon a preacher stands in a modern pulpit proclaiming the modern message, "I'm OK and you're OK" and the enthusiastic congregation responds, "Amen brother, you're OK and we're OK." That captures the prevailing spirit of our time. But that is not the message coming from Calvary. There we read about "darkness over the earth" and the uncomfortable message that so often we inhabitants of the earth vote for the darkness.

The failure of our time to recognize the depth and intensity of darkness is a dangerous miscalculation. Where positive thinking abounds so does unrealistic optimism and the cheap hope that sin will disappear into nothingness. But such shallow thinking knows little about who we really are and it certainly flies in the teeth of the historical record.

Another sobering book that illustrates this uncomfortable truth is, *The Mountain People,* by Colin M. Turnbull.[3] Here we have described the dehumanization of an African Tribe, known as the IK TRIBE. In less than three generations this group of prosperous hunters deteriorated into scattered bands of hostile people. They became brutish, totally selfish and loveless. "They breed without love or even casual regard. They defecate on each other's doorstep. They watch their neighbors for signs of misfortune, and only then do they laugh. In the book they do a lot of laughing, having so much bad luck." So comments Lewis Thomas in his book, *The Lives of a Cell.* It is Mr. Thomas's theory that the Iks have gone crazy, that each Ik has become a group. It is his belief that nations are the most Ik-like of all. For total greed, there is nothing to match a nation. The Lesson? "We haven't learned how to stay human when assembled in masses. Nations have themselves become too frightening to think about."[4]

But it seems that each generation must learn this lesson anew. The monsters are not just in Washington, or Moscow or Peking. They are here, inside of you and me, waiting for the right circumstances to break through the constraints of justice and mercy.

Today we are at Calvary. It is not comforting to stand beneath the Cross and see revealed there our own selfishness and pride. But where the world would offer a slogan or a tranquilizer, the Cross is more honest and says, "As good people drove Jesus to his death, so also the radical nature of sin within us still has the power to make us hate, persecute and kill."

The Cross shows us the truth about ourselves, but it also makes it possible for us to accept this uncomfortable truth. The Cross reveals not only the darkness of our sin, but also the great love of

God. Into our darkness comes the great Light. Through the pain comes the healing. "Father, forgive them, for they know not what they do." (23:34)

"He has delivered us from the dominion of darkness and transferred us to the kingdom of his beloved Son, in whom we have redemption, the forgiveness of sins." (Colossians 1:13)

Amen

1. William Sheridan Allen, *The Nazi Seizure of Power,* (New York, Franklin Watts, Inc. 1984), p. 183.

2. Frederick W. Danker, *Jesus and the New Age,* (St. Louis, Clayton Publishing House, 1972), p. 235.

3. Colin M. Turnbull, *The Mountain People,* (New York, Simon and Schuster, 1972).

4. Lewis Thomas, *The Lives of a Cell,* (New York, Bantam Books, 1975), pp. 126-129.

Lift Up Your Hearts!

Deep within the heart of the Christian faith there are two simple, yet profound and mysterious acts that demonstrate God's activity in our lives. Although there is no universal agreement among the various Christian denominations as how these acts are to be understood, there is general agreement that they are distinguishing marks of the Christian Church. One of them normally happens near the beginning of one's life and is usually never repeated. The other generally occurs after the infant years and is often repeated. The first of these gracious acts is Baptism; the second is the Lord's Supper.

According to Church definition, these acts are called Sacraments. A Sacrament is a sacred act whereby we believe that God comes to us. We also believe that through the power of the Holy Spirit, God communicates his presence to us through the spoken word. In many respects words remain the clearest symbols which we can use to share the good news of God. But they are not the only means, methods or vehicles of grace that God has given us. There are numerous times in life when actions speak louder than words. Dr. Reinhold Niebuhr, a leading theologian and preacher during the middle years of this century, did not have a low estimate of the ability of words to communicate. Yet, after suffering a stroke, he preferred to receive the gospel of God's great love through the Holy Supper, rather than hear someone preach about it. He liked the directness and the reality of the sacrament. In the sacrament of the Supper we are talking about a different kind of experience than that which just comes through our ears. The Sacraments "make the good news of God's love visible, tasteable, feelable." It touches and influences our heart and soul in ways that are unavailable to the spoken word.

Somewhere I read this story: In 1945, just after World War II, there was a meeting of church people in Geneva, Switzerland. Among the people invited were Bishop Berggrav of Norway and the German pastor, Martin Niemoller. Berggrav was a Norwegian who had just spent a long time in a Nazi prison in Norway. Pastor Niemoller was much worried how he would be able to meet this person who suffered so much from the Nazis. How would he react to a German? As soon as Niemoeller came into the room, old Bishop Berggrav went up to him and embraced him. The powerful visible word was in that instance more meaningful than the spoken word.

It seems appropriate in this Maundy Thursday service to share this kind of brief catechetical review of our understanding of the sacraments of the Church, for once again the great Jewish religious festival is at hand. The faithful people of God are coming together to remember and to celebrate God's Almighty act — the Exodus from Egypt.

The underhanded plotting has been accomplished to deliver Christ into the hands of his enemies. But while all of this was going on, Christ was making preparations to celebrate the feast of love and fellowship. Early in Luke's gospel we were told that "Jesus set his face to go to Jerusalem. And he sent messengers ahead of him." (9:51) Now the final hour was at hand and once again messengers were sent on ahead. Peter and John, who were with him for that mysterious Transfiguration experience, were chosen to make ready for the climactic event that is at hand.

When the hour had come and Jesus sat down to the prepared meal, he said, "I have earnestly desired to eat this passover with you before I suffer." (v. 17) It is not clear why, in Luke's account of the Lord's Supper, the Supper begins with the wine and not the bread. Some believe that we have recorded here two "distributions" — the first commemorating the Passover and the second (v. 20) instituting the "new" supper. There is much to commend this interpretation, but a sermon is not the place for this kind of study. This much is clear: this is a solemn moment. Jesus will celebrate no more Passovers with his friends. It is with desire that he wants to eat this final meal together. It is also clear that the final supper is specifically linked to the Passover festival. The purpose of this connection seems obvious. The time has come when Jesus will depart this life. It will be his "Exodus" happening in that time when people are remembering their first Exodus from slavery in Egypt.

The drama is unfolding which will reveal another great action on the part of God. The first recorded act was the Exodus from Egypt and God's people living in the "promised land" of Palestine. It was the time of the "law and the prophets;" the time of the promised new covenant (Jeremiah 31:31-34); the time which culminated in the preaching of John the Baptist and the coming of the promised Messiah. "In the fullness of time", God sent his Son. This is the second phase in the history of our salvation. With Christ's coming, the Kingdom of God has been ushered and begins to take shape and grow. The third stage or phase in our human understanding of this "plan" of salvation is that of Pentecost, when the Christian Church was born with the Spirit of the Risen Christ in her midst, in and through the Word and Sacraments. This is the age in which we are living. It is the living in the Kingdom "in-between-the-times," looking forward to that final phase when God's kingdom will come in all of its fullness and completeness. In this solemn moment when God's people come together to remember the first Exodus, and just hours away from Jesus' Exodus, we have a moment which is connected with what God has done, what he is doing and what he will do. The meal belongs to this climactic moment.

These are some of the reasons this Maundy Thursday Holy Communion Service holds a special place in our lives. It is why the time-honored words, "In the night in which he was betrayed, Jesus took bread" usher in for us a solemn and emotional moment. Here in this solemn moment we experience something of that "cloud of witnesses" which surround us, those who participated in this meal before our generation. We go back to that "moment when he was betrayed" and the Passover Celebration and what we Christians owe to our Jewish roots. We go back and, with death near at hand, hear once again the time-honored words, "it is with desire that I want to eat this supper with you."

In one sense this desire is surprising. Jesus' friends were not the most faithful followers. They never did understand his ministry and they certainly don't understand what is now happening. They are still proud. They are still bickering among themselves as to who is the greatest. They have no great degree of confidence in Christ. Later on they deny him and leave him. They are not exactly the kind of people with whom you would want to spend your last hours — yet

Christ has a burning desire to eat and drink with his spiritually-poor friends.

But of course, we shouldn't be surprised. God didn't send his Son to strike terror in our hearts. He sent his Son because he loves us and desires our salvation. This last hour and Last Supper is a time of encouragement and assurance, not a time of scolding and condemnation. Holy Communion is a time when "hearts are to be lifted up."

So we too are welcomed to this sacred feast. No matter what our spiritual condition, Christ, who longed for communion with sinners and outcasts, with a dying thief on the cross, also earnestly desires communion with you and me. "Lift up your hearts!" There is a love here that we can never understand or fully explain. There is a love here that never wearies of giving, that is in fact always seeking ways to give. If it is with any sort of desire that we want to be here, it is because of Christ's deeper desire. In this gracious supper, to which we come as invited guests, our Host is saying to you and me, "Come, no matter what your condition, no matter what your feelings. Come, I still believe in you. Come, you can become whole, holy, free from slavery to things and events that make life hell. Come, I will deliver you." This is his gracious invitation. He is the host, we are the guests and the main message of all of this is one of assurance. Se we can "lift up our hearts."

But in this quiet supper with his friends, Jesus' words of farewell promise even more. He pledged to them, "For I tell you that from now on I shall not drink of the fruit of the vine until the kingdom of God comes." (v. 18) Here the Holy Supper stretches forward into the future. As we come to the Supper this evening, may we remember this forward looking view. For many of us, partipation in the Lord's Supper is a family affair. When husband and wife commune together for the first time, that is a memorable occasion. When children join us at the table for the first time, this too becomes one of those treasured moments. But the time eventually comes when, instead, of additions, there will be subtractions. Some now commune alone, who but a short time ago did so in the company of loved ones. For such ones the future aspect of the Supper takes on an even more significant and gracious meaning. Here is our living hope. Christ and his people will be gathered into one home. We eat and drink at this table assured of eternal life, which beginning in time cannot be terminated by death.

On the night in which he was betrayed, our Lord had supper with friends and promised those friends another supper in the future. He has had many suppers since, but the final one is coming, when separations will be no more and all tears will be washed away. This is Christ's promise in his Supper. We do not know the time of that final coming, but we do know who is coming. It is the one who meets us in this Supper and who will meet us in the end — Jesus Christ, our Lord. Lift up your hearts!

Amen

It Is Finished

Among some Christians a favorite question for speculation and discussion is the activity and whereabouts of the devil. The answer that is useful to me is this one: "If you want to catch the devil, I am going to tell you where you will most surely find him — seated in your own arm chair if in it you are alone!"

Such is the reason and realism of Good Friday. Jesus died on the cross because his life was on a collision course with the powers that be. He antagonized the religious establishment. This created the possibility of civil unrest which prompted fear in the heart of the government. One can hear the justifying process: "What should we do? If we let him go on in this way, everyone will believe in him and the Roman authorities will take action and destroy our Temple and our nation." Such is the realism of this tragic event. And it is scary! For the powers that be were made up of well-meaning people; people who honored age-old traditions; people who respected their institutions; people who wanted to protect their own way of life. The cross of our Lord clearly but uncomfortably demonstrates the evil that is alive in the heart of what we call goodness or respectability.

Even this very Gospel is evidence of what we are talking about. For here the Jewish leaders bear more responsibiiity for Jesus' death than the Roman Government. Consequently, down through history it has been the source of vicious and unbelieveable persecution of Jews, much of its ugly head revealed on Good Friday.

And in various ways we conveniently rationalize our decisions. We are sincere when we say, "It is too bad that in the economic readjustment that needs to happen, the poor have to suffer." We contemplate the fate of the refugees in similar fashion. "It's not their

fault, but we just don't have any more room, nor any more jobs."
And that is how Mr. Evil does his work — not in other people, but
in me.

"If Russia would just be a Christian nation . . ."

"If people wouldn't be so greedy. . ."

"I don't want that people should suffer. . ."

"It's too bad." "It is unfortunate." "I wish the world were not
like this." "But since it is, this is probably the best way in the long
run."

"It is expedient . . ."

The Good Friday tragedy is the eternal reminder that evil is real,
that Pilate is every person, and that the religious establishment is
every person. The words in John 10:33 shed significant light on the
Good Friday event: "We do not want to stone you because of any
good deeds, but because of your blasphemy."

But the lesson of realism is not one of pessimism. John does not
minimize the power of evil that put Jesus on the cross. Still, for him
this is not the most important word and certainly not the last word
from the cross.

For in John's description of thae crucifixion, evil did not win
the day. Jesus did not die as victim, but as victor, not as a helpless
sufferer, but as king. It is in this insight that John's carefully crafted
Gospel and account of Jesus' death is so strikingly different from
the other evangelists.

At each step of the way Jesus is in charge. His arrest is described
in this fashion: "Jesus knew everything that was going to happen
to him, so he stepped forward and asked them, 'Who is it you are
looking for?' 'Jesus of Nazareth,' they answered. 'I am he,' he said."
That is not the response of a frightened person being dragged to the
sacrifice!

Or again, consider how he responded to the charges by the high
priest: "If I have said anything wrong, tell everyone here what it
was. But if I am right in what I have said, why do you hit me?"
One wonders who is really being questioned!

Once more, notice the direct words to Pilate: "You have authority
over me only because it was given you by God." Not exactly the
words of a helpless victim, would you say?

From John's perspective of the cross, Jesus is in charge. Each
step of the way it is he who takes the initiative. He carries his own
cross to the place of crucifixion. And there is no mention of any

help or any stumbling along the way.

Friends, there is something more happening here than just an unfortunate accident. There is something more involved here than just bad timing by the forces of history. Nor is the cross of Christ simply the focusing point of demonic sin. That something more Jesus made very plain when he announced to his disciples, "No one takes my life from me, but I give it up of my own free will."

So the cross was not forced upon him. He willingly accepted it. He did not lose his life. He gave it. He was not killed. He chose to die.

But is that all that is going on here? A good person who is perhaps a deluded fanatic going willingly, knowingly and bravely to an agonizing death?

Early in the Gospel, John the Baptizer points up the purpose of it all when he points out the Christ and says, "There is the Lamb of God who takes away the sin of the world."

And there you have the reason for the crucifixion.

But John is not content just to say it. In characteristic fashion he calls attention to our struggle with evil by highlighting it through such motifs as darkness versus light; seeing versus believing; judgment versus eternal life. In all these descriptive and helpful comparisons he never loses sight of the Cross. In John's Gospel the Cross has the center stage. The Cross is the hour that has "yet not come" but for which Jesus was preparing. This was the hour about which Jesus could say, "Father, save me from this hour," and yet in the same breath say, "For this cause I came to this hour."

This "hour" language vividly dramatizes the sense of divine purpose that had been the reason for Jesus' coming, and for his life. "I am telling you the truth," he says, "a grain of wheat remains no more than a single grain unless it is dropped into the ground and dies."

No, Jesus' death did not come about by chance or bad luck. Rather his death was the aim of his life. It is in this death that the real purpose of his life is revealed.

"The Lamb of God who takes away the sin of the world!"

It is good news that John's Gospel builds this truth carefully and plainly. But it is also a central biblical truth. We can look to the Christmas story, where we hear the news, "You shall call his name Jesus, for he shall save the people from their sins;" or to the Apostle Paul, who preached to the Corinthians, "I delivered to you first of all that which I also received, that Christ died for our sins according to the Scriptures."

Here is the purpose of the Cross: the Good Shepherd giving his life for the sin of his people.

And that is why this Friday can be called "good." Here is the redeeming sacrifice. Here is the sacrificial Lamb. Here is the Good Shepherd who did not leave his flock, even in the face of death. This is what the cross is all about.

In these tragic events our God is at work. Against the dark background of evil the light of unbelieveable love shines forth. Yes, the enemies of God become the means by which his purpose is fulfilled.

"It is finished."

These are Jesus' last words before he died. They are a quiet statement of victory; Jesus is not just saying that his life is about to end, but with the ending of his life, his work is completed. Here is the announcement of the fulfillment of the purpose of this one called Jesus Christ. This is the Christ about whom John said, "Jesus knew that the hour had come for him to go to the Father. He had always loved those in the world who were his own, and he loved them to the very end."

My friends, this news is for you. It is for me. John, more than any other Gospel, wants to drive this point home. This is the tone and tenor of his entire Gospel, expressed most pointedly in his view of Jesus' death. The Cross is the focus of John's Gospel. And he, more than any other Evangelist, helps us to see the Cross through the mind and heart of God.

When you have doubts as to whether or not you are saved, open your Bible to John's account of the crucifixion and read the words, "It is finished." Everything has been done that needs to be done. When some well-meaning but misguided brother or sister hits you with the question, "Are you certain you are saved? Are you really sure?" here is your answer! It is not based on our faith, or feelings which can go up and down like a yo-yo, but on the certainty of Jesus Christ.

Many of us have trouble with this mysterious doctrine of atonement. That may be one reason too many of us are more comfortable with "cross slogans" than we are in trying to understand the various theories of why Jesus had to die. But there is clarity and simplicity in this announcement, "It is finished." Even I can understand that. So can you. This is not a theory. Nor an explanation. It is not a definition.

Here is the announcement, that a task has been completed, and a purpose fulfilled. "Jesus knew that the hour had come for him to go to the Father. He had always loved those in the world who were his own, and he loved them to the very end."

"It is finished."

One thing more. I know you are thinking about it, asking the question that started it all. What about the evil in our hearts? What about the hurts that eat away at us and the fears that overwhelm us and the pervading sense of futility that surrounds us? Is not this Good Friday message just another nice pep talk for Jesus?

We are here on this Good Friday not just because something has gone wrong, but because something has gone *eternally right*. The Cross of Christ was not an accident of history and its victim a helpless pawn. The Cross is the result of God's plan to do battle with the evil of the world and within us. At the cross he tells us that his Son won this war. Yes, we still have to fight some battles. But there is power here to do battle with the evil within us. There is love here that prompts us to question and change our self-serving solutions. Between this hour and the hour when we die, we can live by faith in his declared victory, "It is finished."

---

1. Durwood L. Buchheim, *Augsburg Sermons 2* (Minneapolis, Augsburg Publishing House, 1982), pp. 113-117.

John 20:1-18 (Common)
John 20:1-9 (10-18) (Lutheran)
John 20:1-9

The Easter Hope

One of these days soon I got to face Mr. Death. It's a dreadful thing if you stop to think about it. The most dreadful thing in the world. It's hard to face. It just hovers and we glance at it occasionally.

". . . and we glance at it occasionally."[1] So Karl Menninger, the founder and developer of the world-famous psychiatric center in Topeka, Kansas accurately describes the modern attitude toward death. We may think about it now and then as the years pile up or when we make the appointment for our physical checkup. But we think about it only "occasionally." Death is not a popular topic of conversation, not even in the church. After all, one is supposed to talk about pleasant things. It's difficult to be positive about death. Many believe that our fear of death is the basis for most of our anxiety. Death is a big, big problem. It's a problem that no one can escape. We don't want to talk about it. We want to put it off. But we also know that it is a problem that not one of us is going to get away from.

Today we are going to look at death. We're going to talk about it. We can do this because of Easter. Easter is the anniversary celebration of the resurrection of Jesus Christ. His resurrection means the defeat of death. Jesus did not escape death; he overcame it and became the Lord of death and life.

This good news about death begins with a few friends of Jesus who, on the first day of the week, go to his tomb. No doubt they thought it was all over, these close friends of the crucified one.

Friday's tragedy had shattered their hopes. Shocked and bewildered, they awaited the end of the long Sabbath so they could perform the last sad office for the dead. So, on that Sunday morning in the early dawn, the climax of history — now called Easter — burst upon them.

All the gospels describe this unbelieveable event, which changed the Cross into victory and changed the whole outlook of humanity. Yes, all the evangelists tell the story of the resurrection. But all tell it somewhat differently. John's account seems to be the most unusual of all. Instead of women, we have *a woman* — Mary Magdalene — making the discovery that the stone had been taken away. She brings this disturbing news to Simon Peter and "the other disciple whom Jesus loved." (v. 2) This information is also somewhat puzzling. Generally this unidentified disciple has been thought to be John, the son of Zebedee, who with James and Peter were a kind of special group that was close to Jesus. But we are not sure about this. It is clear that this "other disciple whom Jesus loved" has the better of it in this story. For, upon hearing Mary Magadelene's discovery, the beloved disciple races with Peter to the tomb and he wins the race. But he is quite polite. He looks into the tomb but does not enter. He waits for Peter. And then we have the strange business about the body wrappings and the napkin that had been on Jesus' head. We remember when Lazarus came out of his tomb he was still wrapped in bandages which had been used in preparing him for burial. Here there is no body, but only the wrappings. Maybe it is to show that the body was not stolen (because, had it been, it surely would have been taken wrappings and all). Or maybe the point of these wrappings in the empty tomb is to point up the difference between the resuscitation of Lazarus and the resurrection of Jesus. Lazarus would die again; Jesus will not. But all of this is speculation. All we really know is that the tomb is empty. Since the body wrappings remain, it would appear that this was not the work of grave robbers. But we have no indication as to how the tomb became empty. In none of the gospel accounts do we have an eye witness to the actual resurrection. And we have no attempts to describe it. This "reserve" on the part of the early witnesses is quite remarkable. One would think they would be under a lot of pressure to fill in the gaps, so to speak — that is, to explain, to really clarify what had happened. But this is not the case. In John's account of the resurrection story he focuses upon the "beloved disciple," and when he went in the tomb after Peter and saw nothing but the body wrappings, John tells us "he saw and believed." (v. 8) The story implies that Peter observed but did not understand. However, the beloved disciple saw and believed. It well could be that John is telling us that this disciple who was closest in love to Jesus, the quicker to look for him, also to believe in him, was able to do these things because of his great love for Jesus.

Even though there is no honest way we can resolve the differences or harmonize all of the gospel accounts of what went on that early Sunday dawn, It is clear that the resurrection of Jesus Christ is not an isolated teaching by just a few. The resurrection is important in all the New Testament writings. It's not just the account of an empty tomb, but also a witness to the fact that numerous witnesses also saw the risen Jesus. The earliest testimony we have is that of the apostle Paul who told the Christians in Corinth (who also had a lot of questions about the afterlife):

> *Christ was buried and was raised on the third day in accordance with the Scripture. And he appeared to Cephas; then to the twelve; then he appeared to more than five hundred brethren at one time, most of whom are still alive though some have fallen asleep; then he appeared to James; then to all the apostles; last of all, as to one untimely born, he appeared also to me. (1 Corinthians 15:4-8)*

Not only is this message central to the faith, there is also agreement in the New Testament. Jesus Christ, who died on the cross, did not remain dead. Rather, he is alive and the people who trust in him will likewise live. The risen Christ has become the first fruits of the many who have fallen asleep. This is the meaning of the Easter message and the reason for our Easter hope. For how can there be hope if death is our end? What can we hope for if the cemetery is our final resting place?

However, this hope does not mean we will not have to die. A sign over the graveyard speaks from the dead to the living, "What you are we were but what we are you will be." This is the kind of realism we need to heed. The word of our faith is not that we do not have to die. Neither does Easter mean that we shall avoid the process of growing old and dying. Christ died at the age of thirty-three and we know some die young. And so we must be open to death at any time for we know we will not always be young. And so Easter may not even remove the fear of dying. Dying can still be a painful process which no sensible person would look forward to. And death will still come with some mystery and power. There will still be pain and heartache over the empty place at the dinner table and the one less birthday to celebrate, for no one can take the place of a loved one who has died. Yes, the message of the cemetery remains: "What we are you will be."

But Christ says, "Because I live you will live also." So Easter does not erase death, but it removes the sting of death by conquering it. We can talk about it. We don't have to hide from it or put our hope in heart transplants or a quick freeze. Because of Easter, death becomes the gateway to life. For in the resurrection of Jesus Christ we're not talking about the revival of a corpse or a return to this earthly life only to die again. When we rise with Christ we cross the final frontier of death. Crossing this frontier of death marks the beginning of a new life. It is not like waking in the morning after a long sleep. It is a much more radical transformation than this. We can't even imagine what this new life is going to be like. It defies description pushing our words beyond their limits. The apostle Paul tries to help us understand when he talks about "a spiritual body — a body of glory that is completely different from the perishing body of flesh."

So it's a new life were talking about, a new life with God; life that is complete, not incomplete; life that is not diminished but finished. Hans Kung, a Roman Catholic theologian, tells us this about the new life:

> It would not be a wholly different life if we could illustrate it with concepts and ideas from our present life. Neither sight nor imagination can help us here. They can only mislead. The reality of the resurrection therefore is completely intangible and unimagineable.[2]

There is only one attitude that is appropriate here and that is the attitude of joyful faith. This is the day for joy, this is the day for song.

> Christ has risen! Alleleuia!
> Risen our victorious head!
> Sing his praises! Alleleuia!
> Christ has risen from the dead.[3]

Yes, the discovery of the empty grave announces to us that the greatest enemy of all has at last been conquered. For God did not only roll away the stone from the tomb of Jesus; he also rolls away the stone from the tomb of humankind. Jesus, the Prince of Life, broke the bonds of death. He who died for us now lives forevermore. "Death is swallowed up in victory. Oh death, where is thy sting? Where is thy victory, oh death, where is thy sting?" This is Paul's cry of joyful thanksgiving and it should also be ours, for Easter tells us that there is life on the other side of death Easter tells us that the power of death is not beyond or without the control of God. Easter tells us that the God who loves us so much as to die for us is not going to be frustrated by death. This is the Easter message and the Easter hope. It is the hope for every child of God. Whenever and however death may come, there is another morning — eternal and endless in the heavens for us. This is the good news of the Easter hope. History is not a dreary, endless cycle of sin, suffering, and sorrow. Our faith has a forward looking dimension. Our goal is not the grave but our living Lord with whom we will abide forevermore.

In Jesus' familiar parable of the Lost Sheep we recall the unbelievable devotion of the shepherd to the sheep that was lost. And we remember how the story ended — that delightful and touching picture of the lost sheep on the shoulders of the happy shepherd going home. In that beautiful picture we have the simple but powerful story for all those who live in the faith. We are on the shoulders of the shepherd, going home. All praise and thanks to God!

Amen

1. Karl Menninger, "A Declaration of Minimum Needs for the No-longer-independent Elderly," Des Moines Sunday Register, October 5, 1980.

2. Hans Kung, *On Being Christian,* (New York, Doubleday & Company, 1984), p. 350.

3. "Christ Is Risen! Alleluia," *Lutheran Book of Worship,* (Minneapolis, Augsburg Publishing House, 1978), Number 131. Reprinted by permission.

The Faith Struggle

Let us pray: Lord I believe, help thou my unbelief.

The place is Jerusalem and it is the evening of Easter Day. The message is a virtual replay of what went on in all of our churches last Sunday. We heard the message of hope in God's victory over death. In this instant replay this morning, we hear the same message in Jesus' words, "Peace be with you . . ." (v. 19)

"Peace be with you." So heard the frightened and discouraged followers of Christ who were hiding behind locked doors. Peace for overwhelming feelings of guilt. Peace for the fears that threaten to paralyze them. Peace for the despair that seeks to engulf them.

"Peace be with you." Here are words which briefly but eloquently capture and express the hope of Easter. In my dying moments I would like to think that message will be sufficient — spoken by someone squeezing my hand: maybe my wife, or pastor or friend. "Peace be with you."

So goes the instant replay of last Sunday's message. Now, back to live action. Apparently Thomas was not in church last Easter Sunday. He did not experience what his friends experienced behind those locked doors. Nor is he about to accept their testimony that they had seen the Lord. So today, the Sunday after Easter, the live action zeroes in on Thomas.

> *Eight days later, his disciples were again in the house, and Thomas was with them. The doors were shut, but Jesus came and stood among them, and said, "Peace be with you." Then he said to Thomas, "Put your finger here, and see my hands; and put out your hand, and place it in my side; do not be faithless, but believing." Thomas answered him, "My Lord and my God!" (vv. 26-28).*

John's Gospel is the only Gospel that includes the Easter meeting between Jesus and Thomas. Since his gospel was written some seventy years after that first Easter, there is a strong possibility that neither we nor Thomas are the only ones involved in the struggle to believe. It could well be that the people to whom John is directing his gospel were also growing discouraged and skeptical in the matter of their faith. For one thing, they had expected an early return of their Lord. But seventy years have gone by and nothing has happened. Maybe there wasn't anything to the story of Jesus and his Resurrection. Maybe it had been an invention growing out of wishful thinking.

So the story of Thomas and his now-famous struggle is shared with members of that early church and with us — for the purpose of reassurance.

Many of us are "walking civil wars." We have our days when it is easy to believe. We also have our times when the question returns with haunting intensity! How can we be sure about all this? Are we here because of fear? Habit? Loyalty? My trust in God seems something like March weather, unpredictable and quite changeable. One day it's warm and sunny and the smell of spring and hope is in the air. Life is good. Like makes sense. I've got it together. It's good to be alive. God is like I learned in confirmation class many years ago — gracious and good. But unexplained and unexpected clouds move into my sunny disposition and soon I am experiencing dropping temperatures and snow flurries — or even worse, a mid-western blizzard. My thoughts of June are shoved back to January. My trust in God has taken a nose-dive and, like the thermometer, the bottom has dropped out of my faith and it is just as cold as the weather. For me it is the Easter season, more than any other time, which calls attention to this civil war, this faith struggle within me.

To cope with life, to handle this civil war, some of us listen to the music of yesteryear in order to return to that more favorable climate of the month of June. Others use their bank accounts and go on shopping sprees, travel sprees, dining sprees, spending sprees — any kind of spree to deaden the pain of a dying faith. Others attempt to reduce the pain by turning up the stereo and turning off the world by turning on to drugs and beer. Some of us Christians want an inerrant book to reassure us, or an inerrant interpreter. All of us desire some sign, some clear signal that there is really something behind our every-Sunday-confession: "I believe in God, the

Father almighty, creator of heaven and earth." Or, maybe we decide to give this "God business" one more chance and we strike a bargain with ourselves. For a period of time we are going to be super-active church people. Maybe our confidence in the Lord will be restored by action. Perhaps the coldness of our faith can be warmed up from the heat of our own pious energy.

It is tough to live by trust. We want to live by sight. Jesus' gentle and thoughtful treatment of Thomas and his faith struggle should give us some comfort and courage. Our Lord doesn't slam the door on those who are fighting for faith. But Thomas' struggle points up the need for honesty and realism in regard to our own struggle. If the hope and power of Easter rested completely on the strength and stability of our trust, then indeed there would be little comfort in its proclamation. For it seems that the reality of God and all that that may mean, is never given to us free from doubt, free from questions. Doubt seems to follow faith like a shadow.

We can even argue, at least some of the time, that doubt serves a useful purpose. I read somewhere these words by the respected television commentator, Eric Sevareid: "It is important to retain the courage of one's doubts as well as one's own convictions, in this world of dangerously passionate certainties . . ." There is much wisdom in that observation. I get a bit nervous and would hope God does too, when faith is defined the way one little boy did: "Believing what you know ain't so." We are not to become fanatical and blindly believe that which we know is not true. For, can there not be more real faith in honest doubt than in a Sunday-after-Sunday unthinking recitation of the creed?

So our Easter gospel for this day comforts us with its recognition of the faith struggle that goes on within many of us. But it does not promise an end to the struggle. Our Lord *shows* Thomas. "Put your finger here, and see my hands; and put out your hand, and place it in my side; do not be faithless, but believing." (20:27) From Thomas we hear the strong faith confession, "My Lord and my God!" (v. 28) Jesus responds, "Have you believed because you have seen me? Blessed are those who have not seen and yet believe." (v. 29)

"Happy are those who believe *without* seeing me." This is where we come into the picture. These words are directed to us. For the question remains, "How can one believe in the risen Lord without actually seeing him?"

We know that our faith cannot be turned on like a light switch.

We who are Lutheran learned in Confirmation, "I believe that I cannot by my own reason or strength believe in Jesus Christ my Lord or come to him." Faith is done to me. Faith is the work of the Spirit and it begins in and through my baptism. Faith is a miraculous gift. Yet we know that not all the baptized ones are believers. If we are baptized and faith is a gift, why all our struggles and doubts?

These are "deep-water" questions. We are not going to completely understand the mystery of faith this side of heaven. But I found this insight helpful in regard to my faith struggle:

> *If it is a gift, does that mean that there is nothing we can do about it? Must we say that some people receive it as a matter of good luck, while others miss it through bad luck? Ask yourself how much it depends on you when you fall in love, or when you possess a given talent. Certainly it is false to say that these things are produced by effort. Try falling in love or acquiring artistic talent by effort some time. But it is equally false to say that what we do makes no difference. A man can turn away from love in order to find a wealthy wife. We can fritter away our abilities instead of bringing them to fruition. Similarly Christian hope comes to us as a gift, but we can turn away from it and we can fritter it away. To accept the gift is to remain faithful through hours of darkness. To accept the gift is to place all our earthly tribulations and triumphs in God's keeping.* [1]

It seems to be the nature of my spirit to demand evidence. Yet it doesn't seem that faith grows strong on just evidence. If we believe in God because he has answered our prayers or has given us good health and much success, we are on shaky ground. The demand for more evidence seems insatiable. Plus the fact that the Bible is full of examples of those who lost everything by believing in and obeying the Lord.

But neither are we entirely without some evidence or signs. The Gospel for today is such a sign. For John is concerned that we hear and believe in Jesus Christ and his death and resurrection. The resurrection really happened. The risen Lord was no spook or ghost. The fact that we come together this morning, some 2000 years after the first Easter, is an additional powerful sign that the story of the Empty Tomb is no fairy tale. Again and again we come to the Lord's Table, believing his living presence will continue to strengthen our weak and trembling faith. Through these means the presence of the Risen

Lord works his way and will in me. Through sermons and the study of his Word I learn something about him. I gain a picture of Jesus Christ. I see in him and his life what life is all about and what I ought to be. I learn something about my own selfishness and greed, and feel the need as well as experience the freedom of his forgiveness. I begin to draw some conclusions and discover that I am living out the faith.

But the faith struggle remains. The bottom line still means the "leap of faith." Stumbling blocks to faith can be removed, doctrines clarified and our faith cultivated and stimulated. But the tension between our "yes" and "no" to Jesus remains. Our security, our certainty rests in the *promise of God*. As Christians we continue to live by hope and not by sight.

> *If we want more security than the promise of God, we will have to exchange it for an idol that promises instant salvation. We live by hope or we live by sight, and there is no right way of synthesizing them.*[2]

But it is hope, which ebbs and flows; this hope which has its days and nights; this fluctuating hope nevertheless rests in and on a God who is faithful and a God who is certain. He also has confidence in us for he believes we are capable of that which he requires.

But the struggle continues. We keep the faith, even in the dark. We continue to believe the end of our struggle is safely in God's hands.

"Blessed are those who have not seen and yet believe."

Amen

1. David Roberts, *The Grandeur and Mystery of Man*, (New York, Oxford University Press, 1955), pp. 82-83.

2. Carl E. Braaten, *The Future of God*, p. 131.

The Call to Mission

"Friend, have you caught anything?"

This question comes in the middle of a strange chapter. John's gospel comes to an end at the end of chapter twenty; but it seems to begin again in chapter twenty-one. In this "epilogue" the center of interest remains Jesus Christ, the Risen One. The reality of Christ's resurrection is emphasized. The text opens and closes with this announcement, but in between these anouncements we have the story of a fishing experience. Seven disciples, led by Peter, make for the Sea of Tiberius and some fishing. In light of their experiences at the empty tomb, this action is somewhat strange. Their fishing is unsuccessful. But upon receiving instruction from shore, they make a huge catch — 153 fish is the exact count! They take their catch to shore where breakfast has been prepared for them by the one they recognized as Jesus Christ.

These are the main themes of this story. But there are also some interesting sub-themes: the continuing interplay between Peter and the Beloved Disciple; Peter's being restored to favor; emphasis upon fishing and the "catch" of fish; the meal of fish and bread with its overtones of the Lord's Supper; and the mystery number "153."

It is a strange chapter, but with John's style of meaning-within-meaning, perhaps it is not as strange as it seems. Coming at the end-of-the-end could be one way to make this symbolism even more striking. As the other Gospels end with their "Go into all the world and make disciples . . . ", so John's Gospel ends with the *call to mission*.

In this call to mission we have Jesus Christ revealing himself as the Risen One. Mission begins with him. In John's Gospel he was the center of the important mission promise, "When I am lifted up, I will draw all people unto me." (12:32)

It has been pointed out that the disciples never caught fish without Jesus' help! In the circumstances of this story, the great catch of fish had more going for it than food for a shore lunch. *It is the symbol for mission.* In and with the power of the Risen Lord, the disciples are to go and "catch people." In this strange chapter there are a variety of issues, but all of them reflect life in the church and all seem to point toward mission.

"Friends, have you caught anything?" Translated into mission terms for our day, this becomes the question, "Have you an evangelism program that is working?" In terms of mission this seems to be testing time for the church. Growing numbers of people believe they can get along without the church. There seems to be a certain weariness concerning the traditional ways of the church. As we feel the pull of this exodus from the church, the anxiety level rises. Besides this faith erosion, religions we have never heard of before are flexing their evangelistic muscles. Our text, with its call to mission, is a timely one. It also carried the important reminder that Jesus Christ is to be the center, focus, and motivator for our missionary activities. Some years ago I heard the late president of our denomination, Kent Knutson, outline the four main resources for mission:

1. The most important resource is the Gospel itself. Without the Gospel we have no mission. The good news of Jesus Christ is the reason for mission.

2. The second important aspect for mission is to know that it is for people. This seems obvious, but too many mission programs never get beyond the self-study phase. First we have to organize. Then we have to get a program. Mission work is "people-to-people" work.

3. The third important thing necessary for mission work is strategy. We do need to do some thinking about where our congregation is going to concentrate its energies.

4. The fourth ingredient, according to Kent Knutson, is money. My money can go where I cannot go. My money can be a missionary where I can't be.

All resources — Gospel, people, strategy and money — are important and necessary. But for my purpose this morning, I want to come to give emphasis to the most vital resource, and that is the Gospel itself.

During the Lenten season, one of these sermons focused on the picture of the "father racing out to welcome his wayward son."

(Luke 15:20) We were reminded that here we have a beautiful, powerful picture of the gospel. For this touching story tells us that God cares for us like the father cared for his son. In our struggle with all the questions that go with living and the questions and doubts about our faith, can we not hang on with this? In my off-again-on-again faith and my up-and-down-again-kind-of-life, I believe that behind it all there beats the heart of God who loves me, as the father loved the prodigal.

Here is our reason and here is the power to be missionaries. Who is in a better place to understand, to identify with the struggles of our unchurched neighbors, than we who know something about struggle? Not only that, but we just live across the road or the next apartment, or the next yard from them.[1] I don't think these people are looking for a memorized speech, theological lecture or a sermon from you. They have had enough trouble with clergy sermons without you getting into the act. You believe the important single thing: you believe God cares for you! Because of this, you are there when your neighbor needs you.

If we believe this about our God, then indeed we have a powerful resource. Its the best news there is. Of course it gets a bit foggy around the edges at times. That seems to be the nature of faith. It carries on a running debate with questions and doubts. But that is one of the reasons we are in church. We are here to have our faith strengthened by being reminded of the presence of the living Christ, and of a homecoming and a God who will never quit on us. But again, this also means we are in the best position to understand our unbelieving neighbor, around whom the fog has really settled in.

So we are not going to come at them like spiritual police. "You are a sinner. You could be saved, if only you would say the right words, join the church and become like me!" That's the "elder-brother approach." It may "scare a few people in," but who can estimate the number it has driven out? Years ago the preacher Harry Emerson Fosdick said these useful words: "You don't convince people music is good by beating them over the head with a baton. You convince them by the excellence of performance and rendition."

Our style of evangelism is shaped and controlled by the good news of Jesus Christ. This means we are missionaries, messengers of the King, who love, who attract, who invite our neighbors to see this Jesus. We are not interested in just a three-visit program but a long-term relationship. We don't want to manipulate our neighbors, we want to minister to them. We want to share with them rather than shock or embarrass them. We want to love them rather than label them. We want to affirm their strengths rather than point out their weaknesses.

Whether we are successful, whether we "Catch anything" is not the important thing. That's the work of the Holy Spirit. The important thing is that we are fishing!

This call to mission, and to be missionaries, receives much support and insight from Luke's account of Paul's conversion. "But Saul, still breathing threats . . . " (Acts 9:1), is a vivid description of his life prior to conversion. It also emphasizes the great changes that Christ brought to his life. Here we have another example of the power of the presence of the Risen Christ. This is the only way we can understand Paul's conversion. In Paul we do not have the conversion of a drunken scoundrel wasting away in some dirty alley. Neither does he seem to be haunted by dreams of a bad conscience as was Luther. Rather, we have the conversion of a devout and disciplined person who loved God's law and believed in keeping it.

The call to mission involves the likes of an impulsive fisherman and an intelligent theologian. It might have been difficult to create an evangelism program that would have appealed to both. But no matter. Christ came to both! He is alive. This is the power behind their conversions.

Living in a time when everything has to be instant and where "success is everything," it is well to ponder the great differences in these conversion experiences. Paul was converted in the midst of persecuting and Peter in the midst of fishing. The only common denominator is that Jesus Christ showed himself to both.

The call to mission does not mean that it is "business as usual." But neither should it mean that we push the panic button when we hear the question, "Are you catching anything?" We have a Word-and-sacrament ministry. It is not a flashy ministry, but it is steady and durable. It is through this ministry that I came to faith and I suspect the same holds true for most of you. Most of us still don't have our act together the way we should. We, too, feel the pull of the world and, through what has been called the "grand orgy of materialism," we attempt to dull the pain of a dying faith. We know something about that. We also know the pull of the world which tempts us to turn off all the questions of life and "just believe!"

Yet through it all, we are pursued by something that will not let us go! Even though we have only known and experienced the good news of Jesus Christ in bits and pieces, it seems we can't be satisified with anything less. Here is that mysterious, haunting and ever-powerful pull of the grace of God. It is this pull of grace that pushes us into the world, so that grace may be shared.

    Amen

1. Durwood Buchheim, "The Call to Mission", *Preaching Helps,* (Chicago, Christ Seminary — Seminex, March 1983), pp. 21-22.

Jesus the Shepherd

"How long will you keep us in suspense? If you are the Christ, tell us plainly." (10:24) This is the central and eternal question about this One called Jesus the Christ. In the opening verses of Matthew's gospel we are told, ". . . and Jacob the father of Joseph the husband of Mary, of whom Jesus was born, who is called Christ." (Matthew 1:16) Christ is a title for the one named Jesus. It is the Greek version of the Hebrew title "Messiah." Christ means Messiah. To call Jesus Messiah means to say that Jesus was the fulfillment of Jewish hope and expectations. The Messiah was the one they waited for, longed for. But was Jesus the Messiah? Jesus faced this question many times. Even John the Baptizer had his doubts. "Are you he who is to come, or shall we look for others."

In our text the question comes during the Feast of Dedication. This feast commemorated and celebrated the purification of the Temple. This came about because several hundred years before the Syrians desecrated the Holy Temple by erecting an idol. In strong, vivid words the prophet Daniel called this terrible act the "abominable desolation." This terrible episode came to an end when Judas Maccabeus drove out the Syrians and a new altar was built and rededicated.

It is at this anniversary celebration where the heated debate between Jesus and the religious leaders continues. John, in his gospel, does not provide us with a description of a "formal trial" as do the other gospel writers. This portion of the gospel before us this morning is as close as John comes. It is sufficient. The setting is not a courtroom but it is a trial. For we have here no friendly theological discussion. It is one of those situations in which we sometimes find ourselves — when our questioners are more interested in gathering evidence against us than in clarification of understanding of the issues. They expect to convict Jesus on his answer to the question, "If you really are the Messiah, tell us so in plain words." (10:24)

It isn't as though they haven't received some strong hints as to some possible answers. At Jacob's Well, the woman from Samaria had questions about the coming Messiah. To her Jesus responded, "I who speak to you am he." (4:26) The man cured of his blindness was asked by Jesus if he believed in the Son of man. The man answered, "And who is he sir, that I may believe in him?" Jesus said to him, "You have seen him, and it is he who speaks to you." (9:37-38) But these answers were not suffciently clear nor unambiguous for his questioners. They wanted a clear "yes" or "no."

I, too, wish that Jesus would have given a clear, explicit and understandable answer to this "Messiah" question. I don't suppose it would make much difference in reference to my faith, but I wonder at Jesus' reluctance. It seems he had some concern about wrong interpretations that his answers would bring. Messianic expectations usually moved in the direction of nationalistic, materialistic and political desires. He dealt with those false expectations right after his baptism. In the wilderness he was tested by the devil as to his leadership style and direction. "If you are the Son of God, command these stones to become loaves of bread." Again, "if you are the Son of God, throw yourself down from the pinnacle of the temple." In the last test the devil promised Jesus virtually everything "if you will fall down and worship me." (Matthew 4:1-11) One fears that, in too many situations today, the job of pastor is defined by the expectations of the people. "Whoever pays the piper calls the tune" becomes the basic principle of control in too many congregations. These congregations don't want a pastor who is also their prophet. They want a pastor who is their executive director, someone to keep the "customers" happy. Jesus did not compromise. He did not permit his messiahship to be defined by what the people wanted. He was more concerned with what they needed. It could be that part of our problem with this question, "Who is Jesus?" is that we don't like Jesus' answer.

Another problem might be the sincerity of our question. Do we really *want* to know who he really is? Or do we ask the question because it is the kind of question all half-hearted and half-committed people ask? In our text Jesus gives this insightful response to the burning question: "The works that I do in my Father's name, they bear witness to me; but you do not believe, because you do not belong to my sheep. My sheep hear my voice and I know them and they follow me . . . " (10:25-27) Is not Jesus saying that the reason we are not hearing any answers to our questions is that our questions are not coming from honest hearts? Jesus is not the problem. The problem rests with the listener. So the Apostle Paul warned the Christians in Corinth. The unspiritual do not receive the gifts of the Spirit of God, for such gifts seem foolish to them and they are not able to understand them, because they are spiritually discerned." (1 Corinthians 2:14) So some said he was crazy. Others said he had a demon. Some said he couldn't be the Messiah because he drank too much and ate too much. Could it be that this whole question of Jesus being the Messiah is not so much a matter of definition as discovery, not so much a matter of information as of obedience, more an issue of faith than answers?

Whatever our reasons, it is important to note that Jesus doesn't reject or despise the question. Rather, he encourages our faith by returning to the "shepherd/sheep" imagery — a picture that we all can understand. For references to flocks, shepherds and sheep are many in the Bible, especially in the Old Testament. Are there any more familiar or comforting words in all Scripture than these? "The Lord is my Shepherd, I shall not want." (Psalm 23:1) The prophet Isaiah paints a similar picture of our Shepherd-God in these beautiful words: "We will feed his flock like a shepherd, he will gather the lambs in his arms, he will carry them in his bosom and gently lead those that are with young." (40:11) Jesus grew up with these pictures of God. His thinking about God was formed and shaped in this image of the Shepherd. So, as God's anointed One, he claims the title of Shepherd! He is that shepherd of the Psalms and the Prophets. He is that Shepherd through whom God cares for his people.

He is a shepherd, not a hired hand whose major concern is the pay package and not his flock. He is the shepherd who doesn't stay where it is safe, but rather seeks the lost ones. He is the shepherd who will give his life to save his sheep. "My sheep hear my voice, and I know them, and they follow me, and I give them eternal life, and they shall never perish, and no one shall snatch them out of my hand." (10:27-28)

Even in a technological age such as ours, the picture of Christ as the Good Shepherd remains vivid and understandable. We may not like being compared to sheep. But when you consider their stupidity and stubbornness, it is a comparison that makes sense! My farmer father never cared much for sheep because they seemed prone to sudden mysterious illnesses. They also possessed a contrary spirit that could find a weak spot in the fencing to get out, but never find it again to return home. In his judgment they were prize examples of creatures nibbling themselves lost, far from the safety of shepherd and barn.

But in our text, the center of attention is not the sheep, but the Shepherd. The Shepherd cares for us. The Shepherd risks for us. The Shepherd dies for us. The Shepherd will not let us be taken from him. We will suffer pain and loss and even death as we make our way through the darkness of the valley. But it is the Shepherd's promise that nothing can remove us from his ultimate protection. "Shall tribulation, or distress, or persecution, or famine, or nakedness, or peril, or sword? . . . Neither death, nor life, nor angels, nor principalities, nor things present, nor things to come, nor powers, nor height, nor depth, nor anything else in all creation, will be able to separate us from the love of God, in Christ Jesus our Lord." (Romans 8:35, 38, 39)

Why can the Shepherd make this great promise to his sheep? Because, "I and the Father are one." (10:30) This would appear to be Jesus' greatest claim as well as his clearest answer to the question, "If you are the Christ, tell us plainly." It is also an answer full of good and wonderful news. For if the Good Shepherd and God are as one, it means that our God has all the tender, caring, compassionate characteristics of a good shepherd.

It means that to hear Jesus is to hear God. Jesus' story is God's story. It means the promises of Jesus are the promises of God. If the Good Shepherd and God are as one, it means that our God is tender, caring, kind and compassionate — just like a good shepherd.

Here is good news for the journey we are on. Our Second Lesson reminds us that for many the journey is not an easy one. There is darkness and pain and tears as we continue to make our way. Whether we are young or old we search for some light in the darkness; we cry for some meaning in the suffering we feel and see. Ours has been called a "tear-drenched" world and who can measure the tears that have fallen and are falling? And our anxieties and fears grow with growing doubt about this one called Jesus the Christ.

But he comforts us with the news that he is the Good Shepherd. He reminds us of the great news that the Good Shepherd and God are one. All of this reaches its climax in the Book of Revelation where the promises are fulfilled and the Good News become reality, "For the Lamb in the midst of the throne will be their shepherd, and he will guide them to springs of living water; and God will wipe away every tear from their eyes." (Revelations 7:17)

Who is this Jesus? He is the Shepherd who will guide us and keep us safe. But he is also the Lamb in whose sacrifice we can stand before the throne of God. Who is Jesus? In a variety of images we receive our answers. He is victor and victim, ruler and sacrifice, shepherd and lamb.

Love One Another

The ministry of Jesus Christ, according to John's Gospel, has been compared to the arc of a pendulum. The pendulum begins from its high position with news that "Jesus was in the beginning with God." (1:2) But many preferred the darkness to the light (3:19); and the pendulum reaches its low side with this tragic observation, "Though he had done so many signs before them, yet they did not believe in him." (12:37) The first half of John's Gospel, which biblical scholar Raymond Brown calls the Book of Signs pictures for us the down-swing of our pendulum. The Book of Glory, which is the second half of the gospel, describes the upswing.[1]

But the upswing of this pendulum begins at its lowest point. The hour of Jesus' death is drawing near. There are no more conversations, discussions and arguments with the general public. The time is at hand to prepare his disciples for what is to come. So the first verse of chapter thirteen sets the tone for that which is near: "Now before the feast of the Passover, when Jesus knew that his hour had come to depart out of this world to the Father, having loved his own who were in the world, he loved them to the end." That which is near is made inevitable through the betrayal by Judas. For John ends his description of the Supper and the Foot Washing with this sober information: ". . . Judas immediately went out; and it was night." (v. 30) We are reminded of an earlier warning by John: "We must work the works of him who sent me, while it is day; night comes, when no one can work." (9:14) This "night" or "darkness" imagery is also present in Luke's account of Jesus' arrest: "When I was with you day after day in the temple, you did not lay hands on me. But this is your hour, and the power of darkness." (Luke 22:53)

But in the darkness, the light shines. The moment of Judas'

treachery is the beginning of Jesus glorification. "When he had gone out, Jesus said, 'Now is the Son of man glorified, and in him God is glorified.'" (v. 31) This announcement provides the introduction for Jesus' words of farewell to his disciples. From now on his conversation is directed specifically to the disciples. He is preparing them for his death. "Little children . . . where I am going you cannot come. A new commandment I give to you, that you love one another, even as I have loved you, that you also love one another." (vv. 33-34)

"Little children" — this tender greeting reveals the thoughtfulness and sensitivity of Jesus. He is not projecting a "macho" image nor is he expecting one. It is with the compassion of a parent that Jesus prepares his small family for his death. "Love one another" is the central theme of Jesus' farewell message of support and comfort. It is an important theme for John's entire gospel. It is also a theme which receives much attention and emphasis in the epistles of John.

We are somewhat puzzled that this whole matter of "love" should be introduced as a "new commandment". "What is new about it we ask?" The other question that bothers us is, "How can love be commanded?" The Old Testament contains a number or examples where we are told to love our neighbor. In the other gospels Jesus combines all the commandments into *the* Great Commandment: "And he answered, 'You shall love the Lord your God with all your heart, and with all your soul, and with all your strength, and with all your mind; and your neighbor as yourself.'" (Luke 10:26-27 and Matthew 22:34-39; Mark 12:28-31)

That which is "new" about this love-command is probably the situation. Jesus' death and resurrection are imminent. The new age with new relationships is about to be ushered in through the coming of the Spirit of the risen, living Christ. The "newness" of this command to love is therefore, like the newness of the new covenant promised by Jeremiah. "Behold, the days are coming, says the Lord, when I will make a new covenant with the house of Israel and the house of Judah." (31:31-34)

We certainly had strong hints of this kind of love already in the old covenant. It was in the context of love that God gave the Ten Commandments. But with the life, death and resurrection of God's Son we see this love in its completeness. This is love that comes from the heart motivated by Christ's love. Hence this love is not worried about "how much," nor does it get anxious about who receives it.

For this kind of love knows no limits and it is for everyone. It is love that is spontaneous not mechanical. It is love that is creative and not legalistic. In essence this kind of love cannot be commanded. It must come from within. It is through the indwelling presence of Christ that this kind of love is empowered. It is an imperative that includes the indicative. It is a commandment that is also a gift. Hear again the basis of this gift-commandment: "As the Father has loved me, so have I loved you." (15:9) Here is the source the power to love. In chapter fifteen it is repeated twice and in our text the disciples hear that they are to love one another, even as they have been loved by Christ. (v. 34) Here is New Covenant Love. Just as the branches cannot bear fruit apart from the vine (15:14), so apart from Jesus, his follower can do nothing. But where they abide in him, there will be results — there will be the "works of love."

Another question that has been raised in reference to our text is that it makes no mention of loving one's enemies. Some wonder if love here is not restricted to the small circle of "loving people" who are one's friends. But surely that is to make its application to narrow. We know that the purpose for Jesus' coming was that God might demonstrate his love for all the world. (3:16) It is true that Christians are to love one another, but not as a way of escape nor because it is "safer." That would be a selfish interpretation which utterly betrayed the kind of love whereby Christians become Christians, namely the love of Christ. "Love one another" is the love that holds Christians together. It is their distinguishing mark. Their mutual love for one another is their mark of identification. Love for one another shapes and forms the Christian congregation. In this new commandment the love for neighbor and love for enemy come together. It is the way Christians are to measure their love for God. Hear from one of Luther's sermons, his strong, clear words on the subject of love:

> God does not say, "Thou shalt love the rich, the powerful, the learned, the holy." No, the free love and the most perfect commandment does not apply to such special person, but it knows no consideration of person at all. It is the false, carnal love of the world which looks only to the person and loves only so long as there is profit and hope. When hope and profit are gone, then love disappears also. But the commandment demands free love for everybody, whoever he might be, friend or foe. This love does not consider its own reward or its own good but rewards and does good.

For that reason it is most active among the poor, the needy, the evil-doers, the sinners, the insane, the sick, and the enemies. Confronted by these people this love has the opportunity to suffer, bear burdens, serve, and do good. This keeps love busy, always and everywhere. And note how this commandment makes us equal before God and suspends all differences of calling, person, rank and work. For since this commandment is given all men everywhere, a king and prince (if he claims to be a human being) must confess that the poorest beggar and the leper are his neighbors and he is equal before God. Therefore he does not only owe him help but according to this commandment he must serve him with everything he has and does.[2]

It is also this kind of love that enables Christians to be effective and faithful in their mission. "By this all people will know that you are my disciples, if you have love for one another." (v. 35)

Verse 35 says that even outsiders will recognize the distinctiveness of Christian love. The same theme is found in 17:23 where it is said that the world's attention will be caught by the love and union that exists between the Father, the Son, and the Christian disciples. Such a love challenges the world even as Jesus challenged the world, and leads men to make their choice for the light. Thus, as long as Christian love is in the world, the world is still encountering Jesus.[3]

These words by Raymond Brown are instructive for us as we Christians think upon these farewell words of Jesus to his disciples. We know that the word *love* and its meaning has come in for more than its share of cheap shots. (I sometimes think we make as much fun about love as we do preaching!) We pay a kind of lip service to the whole idea of love but "everybody knows you really can't take it too seriously."

We need to hear again that, for Jesus Christ, love is not simply one virtue among many others from which we may choose, rather it is the foundation, the basic yardstick for all norms and forms of how to behave and act toward one another. Nor is it some kind of cozy relationship between God and me. It is not *feeling* or *sentiment* but rather *action* about which Christian love is concerned. It is "doing good" for others. It is an attitude with guides, instructs and regulates our action toward others. According to Jesus, "loving one another" is to be the most distinctive characteristic of our Christian congregations. And John's Gospel is not the only place we hear about it. We read the admonition in Ephesians, "with all lowliness and meekness, with patience, forbearing one another in love, eager to maintain the unity of the Spirit in the bond of peace." (4:2-4) Congregations are to be those communities where we build one another up instead of tearing them down. In First Peter we read, "Above all hold unfailing your love for one another, since love covers a multitude of sins." (4:8) Again, Paul's words to the Christians in Thessalonica: "We are bound to give thanks to God always for you, brethren, as is fitting, because your faith is growing abundantly, and the love of everyone of you for one another is increasing." (2 Thessalonians 1:3)

This is what Easter is all about. Eternal life is not just something that happens when we die, but is present now. This is what it means to live in the spirit of the risen Christ. It means a radical orientation of our life. It means newness of social life, since there is no other kind of human life. The first and all-inclusive result of "walking in the Spirit" is the visibility of our love. It means that we who have received the Gospel of Jesus Christ have received his love and with it the "new command to love one another."

"With Christ have I been crucified, and so I live. Yet it is no longer I, but Christ who lives in me. And this life which I now live in the flesh, I live by faith in the Son of God who loved me and gave himself for me." (Galatians 2:19-20)

Amen

1. Raymond E. Brown, *The Gospel According To John XIII-XXL,* (New York, Doubleday and Company, 1970), p. 541.

2. Martin Luther, translated from the *Weimar Edition of Luther's Works.* Quoted from George Forell, *Faith Active in Love* (Minneapolis, Augsburg Publishing House, 1954), p. 104. Reprinted by permission.

3. *Ibid.,* Raymond E. Brown, p. 614. Reprinted by permission.

We Are Not Alone

The term "Holy Spirit" has become a kind of catch-all-phrase where we place all those aspects of the faith we don't understand. He becomes a scapegoat for sloppy thinking and lazy efforts. In this understanding we preachers invoke the Spirit in this fashion. "I preach the Word of God. If the people don't understand it or heed it, it is not my fault!" The implication is that it is either the fault of the Spirit or hard hearts. Or, if we face a tough decision; or we are in the middle of a controversy; or we don't know the answer to some problem or issue — the frequent response is: "Leave it to the Spirit!" It would seem that we can make the Spirit into whatever is convenient or necessary.

> *In this way the Holy Spirit increasingly became a mysterious power through which the otherwise incomprehensible, and indeed even the absurd, is nevertheless to be legitimated . . . We may well ask ourselves whether this was not an all-too-easy way of escape from the questions which faced the Christian message — the question of what was really true. And has the Christian doctrine of the Holy Spirit not been misused and discredited because it has been used as a fig-leaf to protect the nakedness of the Christian tradition from the questionings of modern critical thinking?*[1]

We know that our church history records a number of evil things done in the name of the Spirit. There are people who claim special appearances of the Spirit. Some are naive and confused Christians. Some are charlatans who desire to exploit people. I have been in conflict situations where people have told me that, while reading the Bible the Spirit had told them it was time for their pastor to resign! Is this how the Spirit works?

Besides all these questions, some of us wonder why our Christian lives are so ordinary and routine and even boring. Why don't we experience more of the "spirit" that other people talk about. The prayer in the Old Testament remains a vital one for many of us:

Create in me a clean heart, O God,
and put a new and right spirit within me.
Cast me not away from thy presence,
and take not thy Holy Spirit from me.

(Psalm 51:10-11)

Our Gospel reading comes from the lengthy farewell speech of Jesus at the Last Supper. The atmosphere is one of confusion and fear. The main topic of Jesus' speech is the Holy Spirit. Immediately one thing becomes clear: Jesus is leaving, but we are not left alone. "These things I have spoken to you, while I am still with you. But the Counselor, the Holy Spirit, whom the Father will send in my name . . . " (v. 16) We have God the Father sending the Son. In Jesus' life on earth we learned about God. This work has been completed. But God did not leave us empty and alone. We are told in our text that God, the Father will send the Spirit. God remains present in our lives through the experience of the Spirit.

The close relationship of God, Christ and the Spirit is clear. The Spirit of God, the Spirit of Christ is the ongoing and contemporary presence of Christ.

As Spirit of God and of Jesus Christ for me he is never identified
with man's own possibilities, but is force, power and gift of God.
He is not an unholy spirit of man, spirit of the age, spirit of the
Church, spirit of office, spirit of fanaticism, but is and remains
the Holy Spirit of God who moves where and when he wills and
does not permit himself to be used to justify absolute power of
teaching and ruling, to justify unsubstatiated theology, pious fan-
tisism and false security of faith.[2]

The Spirit comes through God's Word. He does not add anything to God's Word. The Spirit does not bring new revealed truths about God. This is one reliable guide to "test the spirit."

Beloved, do not believe every spirit, but test the spirits to see whether
they are of God; for many false prophets have gone into the world.

*By this you know the Spirit of God: every spirit which confesses
that Jesus Christ has come in the flesh is of God, and every spirit
which does not confess Jesus is not of God. (1 John 4:1-3)*

If at times we are confused as to whether or not it is our spirit,
or the emotional moment, or the spirit of a high-powered evangelist,
we have this simple and helpful test to guide us. Is what we are experiencing or hearing consistent with the message and life of Jesus
Christ?

So we are not alone. The Divine Spirit is in our midst. The Greek
word is the word "parakletos." There are various English transla-
tions for this word. The Spirit is our "helper" or "comforter." This
is not to be interpreted as a kind of "security blanket" or some mag-
ical power that will protect us from all harm or get us through life
without trouble. To be filled with the Spirit is not to be wrapped
in a warm, cozy blanket.

The presence of the Spirit in our lives enables us to cope with
what life delivers to us. This is a more realistic understanding of the
Parakletos. When our life threatens to get out of control, or be over-
whelmed by circumstances and events, it is our Lord's promise and
the power of his Living Spirit that enable us to pick up the pieces
and to once again see our life with meaning and purpose. God does
not leave us alone. The Parakletos is with us — as Comforter, Helper
and Counselor.

One of the ways in which we are helped by the presence of the
Spirit is this: "He will teach you all things, and bring to your remem-
brance all that I have said to you." (v. 26) "All that I have said
to you" reminds us again of the relationship between the work of
the Spirit and the teachings of Jesus Christ. But in the vernacular
of our time, the Holy Spirit will help us to "get it together" — this
whole business of what it means to be a disciple of Jesus Christ.
Later on in this goodbye speech, Jesus calls the coming Spirit "the
Spirit of Truth" and says to his disciples, "When the Spirit of truth
comes, he will guide you into all truth." (16:13)

One of the great challenges our government faces today is that
of credibility. Few of us take at face value any statements that come
from the White House or from Congress. The problem is not new
and it is not located just in Washington. It is worldwide. Because
the problem of truth is so extensive and deep, a growing cynical spirit
pervades our time and our land. We just *expect* to be lied to — if

not all the time, at least most of the time. It might as well be all the time, for it becomes increasingly difficult to sort out the truth. So today, much of our serious conversation ends with: "What can you believe? What can you believe?" In the eighth chapter of John's Gospel, Jesus says these words: "If you abide in my word, you are truly my disciples and you will know the truth."

We don't always understand or recognize the truth. We need help. The truth needs additional "light or illumination:. Or, if we *do* understand the truth it may not be able to penetrate our greed and prejudices. The "old nature" in us has many ways of filtering out truths we don't want to hear or follow. For these truths to reach us inwardly and to overcome our deeply-rooted prejudices, we need the Spirit of truth teaching and reminding us of "all that Jesus has said and done for us." Again we are not talking about new truths or teachings, but through the Spirit of Jesus, his teachings become for us a new reality. The once-for-all teachings of Jesus Christ unfold for us in the ever new understandings, ever new interpretations, ever new ways of living the Christian life.

Our lives don't always reveal that they have been taught by the Spirit. The presence of the Spirit does not put us into the delightful land of bliss and happiness. This calls for some humility on our part as we interpret the work of the Spirit in shaking and shaping our lives. There is mystery here. There is also our own sinfulness which continues to complicate and confuse our thinking and understanding. The clear, blunt words of George Sweazey are instructive here. He writes in his book, *In Holy Marriage,* concerning the power of the Evil One and the alluring disguises of lust: "A man getting into a sordid affair tells himself that he is impelled by tenderness and sympathy and spiritual affinity. Temptation gets at us through our virtues. Religious people readily mistake their hormones for the Holy Spirit."[3] But in spite of all the problems and difficulties, in spite of what we see or don't see in our lives in reference to the Spirit's presence, we have the promise and we hold fast to that. The Spirit has been given to us. We are not alone. We belive he continues to teach us — to lead us into all truth through the foolishness of what is going on here at this moment. Through the means of grace — The Word and Sacraments — the Spirit of Christ continues to shape us. Through these means the Spirit brought us to faith. He is responsible for why we are here. Jesus did not leave us alone. He continues to teach us, to lead us into the truth, to hold us fast in the faith.

The result of all this is his peace. "Peace I leave with you; my peace I give to you; not as the world gives do I give to you. Let not your hearts be troubled, neither let them be afraid." (v. 27) In this parting gift of peace, we have a majestic promise. But again we see this great promise in the light of Jesus' life. Hence we know his peace is not necessarily to be understood in the light of "positive thinking" or that we can go through life as always "winners."

> *The peace of which Jesus speaks has nothing to do with the absence of warfare (indeed it will come only after the world has been conquered; 16:33), nor with an end to psychological tension, nor with a sentimental feeling or well-being . . . In Johannine language "peace," "truth," "Light," "Life,", and "joy" are figurative terms reflecting different facets of the great gift that Jesus has brought from the Father to men. "Peace is my gift to you" is another way of saying "I give them eternal life" (10:28)*[4]

This little group of people, hearing the promise of this gift of peace, did not know where it would take them. We know that this peace did not keep them out of trouble or pain. It would seem that many of these early followers died a martyr's death. Yet there is little question that their lives were filled with the peace of satisfaction, purpose and meaning. They had a reason for living. It is in this experience that we begin to understand that "peace which passes all understanding". Martin Luther did not know all the excitement and problems his study, prayer and thinking would get him into. But in and through the struggle came the glimpses and assurances of Jesus' great promise, "my peace I give to you, but not as the world understands it."

Here is peace coming through the promise that we don't have to stay the way that we are. There is power to change. We can get out of our rut. Every day holds the change for newness, for surprises. Because of the power and presence of the living Spirit of Jesus Christ our faith is the faith of new beginnings. Herein lies our peace. So "let not your hearts be troubled, neither let them be afraid." (v. 27)

Amen

1. Wolfhart Pannenberg, *The Apostles' Creed,* (Philadelphia, The Westminster Press, 1972), pp. 130-31.

116

2. Hans Kung, *On Being a Christian,* p. 471.

3. George E. Sweazey, *In Holy Marriage,* (New York, Harper & Row, 1966), pp.73.

4. Raymond E. Brown, *The Gospel According to John XIII-XXL,* (New York, Doubleday and Company, 1970), p. 653.

Luke 24:44-53   *Ascension Day (Lutheran)*
                                     Ascension Sunday (Common)

He Ascended Into Heaven

After hearing the story of Christ's Ascension, a small child responded, "When the Lord Jesus finally got to heaven the Father told him, 'Better stay up here, otherwise something will happen to you again'."[1]

We smile at this immature response, yet there is something refreshingly honest about it. In this day of sophisticated technology, when travel in space is an everyday occurrence, we know there is no "up-or-down" — we don't hear much adult conversation about "Jesus going *up* into heaven and sitting at the right hand of the Father." One hopes this silence about Jesus' ascension comes more from humility than embarrassment. For there is mystery here. We, too, confess with the author of 1 Timothy, "Great indeed we confess is the mystery of our religion,"

> *He was manifested in the flesh,*
> *vindicated in the Spirit,*
> *seen by angels*
> *preached among the nations,*
> *believed on in the world,*
> *taken up in glory. (3:16)*

There we have a brief summary of the mystery of our religions, reaching its climax in the statement, "taken up into glory." But it is a *popular* mystery. There is much evidence that the New Testament accepts the ascension of Jesus as an essential part of the faith. We read about it in the Ephesian epistle: "He who descended is he who also ascended far above all the heavens, that he might fill all things." (4:10) That which prompted the stoning of Stephen were these words: "Behold, I see the heavens opened, and the Son of man standing at the right hand of God." (Acts 7:56) Jesus was probably referring not only to his Cross but also ascension when he said, "I, when I am lifted up from the earth, will draw all people to myself." (John 12:32)

Our text in Luke's gospel says it briefly and simply: "While he blessed them, he parted from them." (v. 51)

There is also mystery as to the time of Jesus' departure. Only in the gospels of Luke and John is the resurrection of Jesus separated from his ascension. The words of the biblical scholar Reginald Fuller are helpful at this point:

> In our Gospel for today it would seem that Jesus ascended on Easter Sunday evening or at the latest the next day. Yet our Epistle lesson from the book of Acts tells us that it was after forty days. In John's gospel, Jesus ascended sometime during the first week after the empty tomb (between his appearance to Mary Magdalene and the appearance to Thomas). It would seem that we observe the Ascension festival on fortieth day as a matter of convenience in order that we might think about it separate from the total Easter event.[2]

However we might explain the when of Jesus' Ascension, it is a well-attested biblical truth that he did leave. It is equally clear that it marks the end of his earthly ministry. Jesus did go away. He told his disciples, "A little while, and you will see me no more; again a little while and you will see me." (John 16:16)

Jesus will not appear to us as he did to the disciples. That which we now call "the time of the Apostles" is over. It was and is basic to the Christian message that Jesus had come down from heaven to live among the people of this earth. He was born of a woman, in a manger's cradle and to the home and work of a village carpenter. He associated with outcasts and sinners. Mockery and scorn were heaped upon him. The ultimate in his humiliation was his death upon the cross. It is Jesus' earthly ministry that provides us with the *content* of the "good news." It also gives our faith a foundation in history. This is what makes the Christian message a message and not a fairy tale. We can point to the Messenger. Our faith is not built upon an idea or accident, nor a myth or legend. "And the Word became flesh and dwelt among us full of grace and truth . . . and from his fulness have we all received grace upon grace." (John 1:14-16) He came down to earth. His life began in Bethlehem and it ended at Calvary. His was a unique life, but on this earth his work is finished. He no longer lives here as you and I live. He is in heaven, but heaven is not some mansion in outer space. Heaven is where God is. The Ascension means that Jesus Christ is no longer here but with God.

One might think this kind of ending would create despair and sadness. But instead of tears we have joy. Our text reads, "And they returned to Jerusalem with great joy, and were continually in the temple blessing God." (v. 52) This was no sorrowful goodbye. Neither do we have any hints that the early followers indulged in any spiritualistic hocus pocus, in order that they might talk to him. No magic potions or drugs were consumed that they might have visions of him. It isn't as though these early Christians didn't care or were indifferent to the earthly presence of Jesus. Quite the contrary. They treasured the moments he was with them. With great care they wrote them down. But it is significant that the Epistles, many of which were written before the Gospel stories, contain little information regarding Jesus' earthly ministry. As has been pointed out, the Apostle's Creed jumps from the phrase, "born of the Virgin Mary" to the phrase, "suffered under Pontius Pilate," thus ignoring most of Jesus' ministry on earth. The early Christians came to realize the presence of the risen Christ as a permanent reality. The Ascension of Jesus, therefore, was a celebration. They celebrated the leaving of Jesus and the coming of his Spirit.

But there is more to it than just a "leaving and a coming" or an "end and a beginning." The thoughts of the respected theologian Karl Barth can help us at this point:

> But what has occurred once for all (Jesus' earthly ministry) now stands rounded off before us in a whole series of perfects; begotten, conceived, born, suffered, crucified, dead, buried, descended, rose again; and now suddenly a present: "He sitteth on the right hand of God." It is as if we had made the ascent of a mountain and had now reached the summit. This present is completed by a final perfect, that he ascends into heaven; which for its part completes the "rose again from the dead."[3]

With Jesus' Ascension, we have moved into a new "time-zone." We live in the "now-time; the in-between-time; the end-time." But there is simply nothing to compare with what we are talking about! In Jesus' Resurrection and Ascension we have the great turning point in history. Barth calls the Ascension of Christ the *conclusion* of Christ's Resurrection. How much of the greatness of this moment the early followers of Jesus comprehended, we can't say. But their mood of exhilaration and joy would indicate that some of it was getting through.

But the "now-time; or the end-time; or the in-between-time" also meant for them *mission-time*. It was the *time of the Church*. The Ascension of Jesus marks the end of his earthly life but it ushers in the mandate for mission. We see this in the familiar missionary command in Matthew's gospel, "Go therefore and make disciples of all nations, baptizing them in the name of the Father and of the Son and of the Holy Spirit, teaching them to observe all that I have commanded you." (28:19-20) In our Gospel text, Luke says it in this fashion: "Thus it is written, that the Christ should suffer and on the third day rise from the dead, and that repentance and forgiveness of sins should be preached in his name to all nations, beginning from Jerusalem. You are witnesses of these things, and behold, I send the promise of my Father upon you." (vv. 46-49)

This is the dynamic aspect of the Ascension. The decisive victory of God has been won at the Cross and the Empty Tomb. We know the outcome of the war, but there are many battles still to be fought. The millenium has not yet been ushered in. Utopia is not around the next corner. But this "interim time" between Jesus'earthly life and his return in glory is *our* time. It is the time of the Christian and of the Church. Karl Barth calls this time of mission "the time of the Word."[4] It is our time of opportunity, our time of mission. The world is not going to hear his Word unless we proclaim it. The world is not going to believe in this Christ unless they see him in our words and deeds. "Church time, end-time, final time — what makes time so significant and great, is not that it is final time but that it leaves room for hearing, believing, and repenting, for proclaiming and comprehending the message."[5]

But our time in the light of Jesus' Ascension is also the time of hope. This is so because it is the festival of Jesus' Lordship. Jesus' humiliation is over. It is now the time of his exaltation. Sitting at the right hand of God means that the risen Jesus is exalted to participate in the almighty power of God — to exercise rule over creation. "Therefore God has highly exalted him and bestowed on him the name which is above every name, that at the name of Jesus every knee should bow, in heaven and on earth and under the earth, and every tongue confess that Jesus Christ is Lord, to the glory of God the Father.'' (Philippians 2:9-10)

We believe Christ is directing the drama of history. As has been said many times, "most of the tapestry that is being woven by his power and love, we see only from the back side, and it is hard to discern its pattern." But we believe there is a pattern. Our hope is directed toward the coming again of the risen Lord to make visible the rule of God which he had proclaimed.

We need to be reminded of this great hope, for too frequently the direction of the world is marked by the prosperity of the godless and the suffering of the innocent, and human conduct becomes a mockery. But his Lordship puts teeth and hope into his saying, "He who rejects me and does not receive my sayings has a judge; the word that I have spoken will be his judge on the last day." (John 12:48).

So we live in between the present rule of the Lord and the final consumation of his kingdom. This means living in between the push of the spirit of the Risen Lord and the pull of that time when he comes again "Beloved we are God's children now; it does not yet appear what we shall be, but we know that when he appears we shall be like him, for we shall see him as he is." (1 John 3:2)

So the heavenly messenger's comment on Jesus' Ascension is pertinent for us: "Why do you stand looking into heaven? This Jesus, who was taken up into heaven, will come in the same way as you saw him go into heaven." (Acts 1:11) There is no time of nostalgia or self-pity. This is our time. This is the time of the Church — the time of mission. This is the time for "loins to be girded and lamps to burn." "If you are risen with Christ, seek those things which are above, where Christ sitteth at the right hand of God." (Colossians 3:1)

Here is the practical, understandable consequence of Jesus' Ascension. We his followers are not to go around wringing our hands about how bad the world is. Rather, we are to be in the world proclaiming and living his lordship.

Let every kindred, every tribe
On this terrestrial ball
To him all majesty ascribe
And crown him Lord of all.[6]

1. Helmut Thielicke, *I Believe,* Philadelphia, Fortress Press, 1968), p. 188.

2. Reginald Fuller, *Preaching The New Lectionary,* (Collegeville, Minn., The Liturgical Press, 1971), pp. 33-34. Reprinted with permission.

3. Karl Barth, *Dogmatics In Outline,* (London, SCM Press, 1949), pp. 124-128. Reprinted wit permission.

4. *Ibid.,* p. 128.

5. *Ibid.,* p. 128.

6. "All Hail the Power of Jesus' Name", *Lutheran Book of Worship,* (Minneapolis, Augsburg Publishing, 1978), # 328. Reprinted with permission.

"... That They May Be One ..."

This is a great moment in John's gospel. Those of us who have heard "goodbye" speeches before, may not be impressed. But this one is different. It is given between two worlds. We are still in the upper room and in the waning moments of the Last Supper. But Jesus is also only hours away from the Cross. Nor is this a usual farewell pep-talk. In fact it is not a talk at all, but a prayer. But here too it is different, because it is not a "give-me" kind of prayer. Jesus prays to his Father that his disciples may stay together, may have joy in their work, even in the face of a hostile world and that they would stay out of the clutches of the evil one. But it is not only for the eleven followers that he prayed. In our text for today, the climax of Jesus' farewell prayer, Jesus prays for the church of the future. That is, he is praying for you and me. "I do not pray for these only, but also for those that are to believe in me through their word." (v. 20)

This is that unique One, who was with God from the beginning, who was involved in the creation of all things, who lives in unity with the Father. This is One who prays for us. This One who was God's messenger, who came with full authority, who is absolutely reliable, who became "flesh and tented among us"(1:14) — this is the One who prays for us. This One, who is "the lamb of God sent for the sins of the world" (1:29), who breaks the power of sin and proclaims, "If the Son makes you free you are free indeed" (8:32) — this one prays for us. This One who was not interested in his own glory but who said, "My nourishment is to do the will of him who sent me" — yes, this is the One who prays for us!

What does he ask the Father on our behalf? Jesus prays to the Father that we might believe; that we would be one; and, that finally we would be with him.

Jesus says, "I pray . . . for those who are to believe in me through his word." (v. 20) Of first and foremost importance is our trust in God. Before we can talk about "oneness" with others we need this personal "oneness" with Christ. So, being found and seized by Christ, which is the heart of our faith-union experience with him, is of the greatest importance. Faith means being a child of God. It is through this trust relationship that I see God and, more important, see what I can become. In Christ this oneness with God is complete and fulfilled. In you and me this oneness is always in the state of becoming.

As this trust deepens and our relationship with God becomes stronger so also our relationships with one another. Maybe one could go so far as to read this section of John's gospel as an equation: The greater distance we are from God, so also our divisions and distance and suspicions of one another. And of course, the reverse would be equally true.

This brings us to the main emphasis of Jesus' great prayer: *future believers are to be one.* This is his prayer to the Father. ". . . That they may be one; even as thou, Father, art in me, and I in thee." (v. 21) Possibly to make sure we don't miss the importance of this unity, the prayer for oneness is repeated in verse 23. Here in Jesus' majestic prayer we have the classic statement concerning Christian unity. In chapter seventeen of John's gospel we have the most explicit central Biblical encouragement for all ecumenical dialogue. These are difficult verses to ignore. We tend to reduce some of their directness by pleading the unity that we already have in Christ.

There is truth here. We rejoice in the growing cooperative spirit that is evident in the numerous dialogues, mergers, and unions. One of the treasured moments in my early ministry was an ecumenical service with the Roman Catholics and all of us singing the great hymn, "Faith of our Fathers." From my past experiences I never dreamed such a service could ever happen. But because it did happen and is continuing to happen, I should never again doubt the power of the Holy Spirit! I don't see how there can be any other explanation. But we still live in many different denominations. The scandalous divisions remain. So the perceptive newspaper columnist, Sidney Harris observes.

If Jesus returned today, it is hard to conceive that he would fit into the pulpit of those churches representing themselves as his disciples. Each sect would find him "unorthodox" in some part, as he was unorthodox in his own time.

Disunity is the image we project to the world. Even worse, it seems we thrive on our differences. Cooperation is a "no-no" and competition is the name of the game. Some years ago, this observation prompted Mark Gibbs to say, "Ideas between churches flow with the speed of cold tar." Lyle Schaller, the Methodist consultant, provides this biting judgment on our cooperatives efforts: "Lack of money is the root of all cooperation!" How difficult it is for congregations to work together, even when our survival depends on it. I suspect the most damaging heresy of our time is not in this area of Biblical interpretation, but the privatization of our faith. This is individualism gone wild. The Apostle Paul tells us, "To each is given the manifestation of the Spirit for the *common good.*" (1 Corinthians 12:7) But for too many of us "common good" means *my* good or "good" for *my* congregation or for the "good" of *my* church.

How should Christians act toward one another? Isn't that the practical question which "unity" presses upon us? Again, the Apostle Paul can give us some helpful insights. To the Christians in Rome he writes, "For by the grace given to me I bid every one among you not to think of himself more highly than he ought to think, but to think with sober judgment, each according to the meaasure of faith which God has assigned him." (12:3) To the Corinthian Christians he says something similiar, in these words: "That none of you may be puffed up in favor of one against the other." (4:6)

Unity does not mean uniformity. The Son has unity with the Father but that doesn't mean sameness. We don't have uniformity in the Bible. John's gospel is not the same as Matthew, Mark or Luke. We have a diversity of gifts as well as identities. Unity in Christ is not a homogenization process which makes us act, think, look and smell the same. Rather, our differences glorify God our Creator. They are intended by God for the building up of the Body of Christ. Differences should be celebrated, not condemned. The power of the Gospel does not come by forcing a "lock-step" mentality, nor through a phony sameness. The power of the Gospel is in its witness to what God has done for us in Jesus Christ, and in the

Bible that witness finds a *variety* of responses.

In this future community for which Jesus is praying, oneness does not mean sameness, but it does mean "love" among the different members. This commandment to love one another is based on the love between the Father and the Son. "As the Father has loved me, so have I loved you. Abide in my love." (15:10; 14:21) This unity for which Jesus is praying is a union of love. It is clear that this unity comes from God and flows through us. This unity expresses both vertical and horizontal dimensions — namely, the relation of believers to the Father and Son and the relation of believers among themselves.

This unity of love, the power of which comes from God, must be visible enough to attract and challenge the world to believe in God. For Jesus does not only pray for unity, he also prays for mission. "I in them and thou in me, that they may become perfectly one, so that the world may know that thou hast sent me and hast loved them even as thou has loved me." (v. 23) Unity and mission — the two belong together. Mission is enhanced where one sees the visible unity of God's people. But we are also told that church unity not only enhances its mission, but is essential to it. While we continue to debate our differences, our culture continues to convert those who are no longer interested in our debates.

Elsewhere John writes, "By this all people will know that you are my disciples, if you have love for one another." (13:55) We are told that our unity is to be visible, which probably means some kind of organizational unity among the various churches "so that the world may believe."

We would wish that Jesus' prayer would have included some specific instructions on how this unity might be achieved. Individual Christians as well as various denominations are discovering that the path to unity is an arduous one. There is much discouragement because of the time and energy that is needed to work through all of the complications. Maybe we all need to catch the vision of Jesus' prayer for unity so that this process is not just the task for an elected few. Is not Christian unity the responsibility of all Christians?

Because of our pride and sinfulness this search for unity may be a never-ending task. But in recent years we have seen the Holy Spirit change organizational structures and create new channels for cooperation and unity. Jesus concludes his great prayer that our unity with the Father and the Son and with one another will be perfected beyond death and this world, where we are free from sin and suspicion and are fulfilled in his glory. "Father, I desire that they also, whom thou hast given me, *may be with me* where I am, to behold my glory which thou hast given me in thy love for me before the foundation of the world." In that great hope we need not become weary in well doing.

Amen

1. Useful to me in developing the unity theme were *These Things We Hold In Common,* edited by Roy Harrisville. In particular the article, "Unity: Our Common Quest," Gerhard Krodel, (The American Lutheran Church, 1980), pp. 45-61.

Raymond E. Brown, *The Gospel According To John XIII-XXI,* (Garden City, New York, Doubleday & Company, 1970), pp. 768-782.